*Problems of Religious Diversity*

# Exploring the Philosophy of Religion

*Series editor:* Michael L. Peterson, Chair of the Department of Philosophy, Asbury College

This is a series of individual volumes on classic and contemporary themes in the philosophy of religion. Each volume introduces, examines, and discusses the main problems and arguments related to each topic. Each book also considers some important positions of major philosophers, offers thoughtful critiques, articulates new positions, and indicates fruitful directions for further investigation.

1 *Problems of Religious Diversity* Paul J. Griffiths

# Problems of Religious Diversity

Paul J. Griffiths

BLACKWELL
*Publishers*

Copyright © Paul J. Griffiths 2001

The right of Paul J. Griffiths to be identified as author of this work has been asserted in accordance with the Copyright, Designs and Patents Act 1988.

First published 2001

2  4  6  8  10  9  7  5  3  1

Blackwell Publishers Inc.
350 Main Street
Malden, Massachusetts 02148
USA

Blackwell Publishers Ltd
108 Cowley Road
Oxford OX4 1JF
UK

*Library of Congress Cataloging-in-Publication Data*

Griffiths, Paul J.
    Problems of religious diversity / Paul J. Griffiths.
        p.   cm. – (Exploring the philosophy of religion; 1)
    Includes bibliographical references and index.
    ISBN 0-631-21149-7 (hardcover) – ISBN 0-631-21150-0 (pbk.)
    1. Theology of religions (Christian theology)   I. Title.   II. Series.
    BT83.85.G75   2001
    261.2 – dc21                                                    2001000956

*British Library Cataloguing in Publication Data*
A CIP catalogue record for this book is available from the British Library.


Typeset in 10.5 on 12.5 pt Bembo
by Best-set Typesetter Ltd., Hong Kong
Printed in Great Britain by MPG Books Ltd, Bodmin, Cornwall

This book is printed on acid-free paper.

*This book is for my teachers,*
*especially Trevor Williams, Richard Gombrich,*
*Minoru Kiyota, Keith Yandell, and Noriaki Hakamaya*

# Contents

# Series Editor's Preface

Philosophy of religion is experiencing a kind of renaissance. From the last quarter of the twentieth century onward, we have witnessed remarkably vigorous activity among philosophers interested in religion. We are likewise seeing college and university students seeking courses in philosophy of religion at an unprecedented rate. To reach this point, philosophy of religion had to weather the harsh and hostile intellectual climate that persisted through most of the nineteenth and twentieth centuries. Absolute Idealism depersonalized deity, naturalism supplanted a religious worldview, and positivism deprived theological claims of cognitive status. Yet, partly because of incisive critiques of these viewpoints and partly because of new, first-rate studies of religious concepts and beliefs, this field of inquiry has once again come to the fore.

The *Exploring the Philosophy of Religion* series, then, comes into a very exciting arena. The books it contains treat some of the most important topics in the field. Since the renewal of interest in religion has occurred largely among Anglo-American philosophers committed to the best in the analytic tradition, these works will tend to reflect that approach. To be sure, some helpful general introductions and anthologies are available for those wanting a survey, and there are many good cutting-edge monographs dealing with technical issues in this burgeoning area. However, the books in this series are designed to occupy that relatively vacant middle ground in the literature between elementary texts and pioneer works. They discuss their stated topics in a way that acquaints the reader with all the relevant ideas and options while pointing out which ones seem most reasonable. Each volume, therefore, constitutes a focused, intensive introduction to the issue and serves as a model of how one might actually go about developing an informed position.

Philosophy of religion is dynamic and growing. The issues it addresses are of primary significance for understanding the divine, ourselves, and our place in the universe. With this sense of magnitude, the present series has been conceived to offer something to all who want to think deeply about the issues: serious undergraduates, graduate students, divinity and theology students, professional philosophers, and even thoughtful, educated lay persons.

Michael L. Peterson
*Series Editor*

# Preface

Many questions of conceptual and practical interest are raised by thinking about religious diversity. This book is intended principally as a map of the territory covered by these questions. It is a guide to what the questions are, and to ways of thinking about and answering them that have proven attractive and interesting to many. It also contains suggestions, recommendations, and arguments as to how these questions are best thought about. Since each question treated is complex, controversial, and possessed of many and deep connections to other equally complex and controversial questions, I don't expect any of the recommendations offered to find wide acceptance; they will have done their work if they provoke further thought and writing on the topic.

Three threads that run through the book deserve brief comment here.

The first thread is an attempt, not often made, to distinguish with as much clarity as possible responses to the questions posed by thinking about religious diversity likely to be congenial to the nonreligious from those likely to be congenial to those with religious commitments. This I take to be important because of the deep differences in the way these questions appear to the two groups; and because of the influential nature of the attempts by the democracies of the late twentieth and early twenty-first century to offer consistently nonreligious (or religiously neutral) answers to the questions of religious diversity.

The second thread is an attempt repeatedly to draw attention to the fact that resolutions of the questions treated in the book, whether proposed by the religious or the nonreligious, always assume and deploy convictions about matters of fundamental philosophical importance. Disagreements about particular solutions to the questions of religious diversity will not be arrived at without attention to these more fundamental disagreements. This is important because it provides a nice

illustration of a general philosophical truth: argumentative attempts at resolution of a particular philosophical problem are most useful not when
they produce agreement, but when they show with clarity how deep the
disagreement really goes.

The third thread is the frequent recommendation of peculiarly Christian responses (responses that rely on Christian assumptions) to the questions of religious diversity. The responses of this kind that I commend and
argue for will not be attractive – and perhaps not even interesting – to
non-Christians; they won't convince all Christians, either. But their presence is required by the book's second thread, since this suggests that any
attempted resolution of the questions of religious diversity cannot avoid
and should not try to avoid deploying controversial assumptions of a philosophically fundamental sort. Since this book is written by a Catholic
Christian, the assumptions of this kind that inform its attempted resolutions are inevitably and properly those of Catholic Christianity. Their presence and use therefore serves as an illustration of the book's understanding
of how the questions of religious diversity inevitably must be approached.
Christian readers can enter more fully than non-Christian ones, perhaps,
into those parts of the book in which specifically Christian positions are
recommended; but non-Christian readers can profit from them as examples of how a religiously-committed person reasons about these matters.

Two practical matters, in conclusion. First, immediately following this
preface is a section in which the book's key technical terms are given brief
definitions and related discursively to one another. They're given in
roughly the order in which they're introduced in the book. You'll find it
useful to read the key terms section through once before you begin the
book, and then to turn back to it at intervals as you need to remind yourself of how a particular term is being used. The key terms may seem
obscure at first reading, but at that point it's meant to serve only as a guide
or template for what's to come. Its terms will become clearer as you read
through the book.

# Acknowledgments

---

The following people have read and commented upon all or part of this book at various stages of its composition: Jeffery Long, Dan Arnold, Kristin Beise (who also helped me find the sources I needed to consult), Gus DiNoia, Thomas Forsthoefel, Mark Heim, Will Kiblinger, Derek Jeffreys, Jared Ortiz, Jerry Walls, and an anonymous reader for Blackwell Publishers. I haven't adopted all the suggestions made (that would have been impossible), but I have learned from them all and am deeply grateful for the collegial spirit shown by those who made them. I'm grateful, too, to students at the University of Chicago (especially those in my classes on religious diversity in 1997 and 2000) who suffered with apparent good will my teaching about the matters discussed in this book. As usual, I learned more from them than they from me. Finally, this book is written for the greater glory of God and at the service of the people of God: Non solum non peccemus adorando, sed peccemus non adorando.

# Key Terms

A *religion* is a form of life that seems to those who belong to it to be comprehensive, incapable of abandonment, and of central importance. It comes in two kinds: the *home religion*, which is the one you belong to if you belong to one at all; and *alien religions*, which are any you do not belong to. It follows that there are *religious aliens* (those who belong to any alien religion), and *religious kin* (those who belong to the home religion along with you). Those who belong to no religion are *nonreligious*; if you are nonreligious then you have no home religion, which also means that you have no religious kin and that all religious people are, to you, religious aliens.

*Religious claims* are propositions about the setting of human life, the nature of humans, or the proper conduct of human life assent to or acceptance of which is required or suggested by belonging to a religion. These claims may be *alien* or *domestic* according to whether they belong to an alien religion or to the home religion. Religious claims may also be *doctrines* (if explicit assent to or acceptance of them is required by belonging to a religion), or *teachings* (if such assent or acceptance is only suggested). A *religious assent* is the involuntary act of taking a religious claim as true (of believing it); and a *religious acceptance* is the voluntary act of entertaining a religious claim, of affirming it or taking it as a guide. Religious claims typically may be true or false; it follows that they may also be incompatible one with another, in the following senses: two religious claims are *contradictory* if both can't be true and one must be; *contrary* if both can't be true and neither need be; *noncompossible* if each prescribes a course of action and it's impossible for one person to perform both.

*Exclusivism* with respect to truth is the view that true religious claims are found only among the doctrines and teachings of the home religion. *Inclusivism* with respect to truth is the view that it is possible that both the home religion and alien religions teach truth; in its *open* variety it affirms the possibility that some alien religion may teach truths not already explicitly taught by the home religion, while in its *closed* variety it denies this possibility.

Those who recommend *toleration* of religious aliens seek not to interfere with them, to let them be; those who recommend *separation* from them want no contact with them of any kind (in which case their *separatist* desires are *total*); or only to limit such contact (in which case their separatist desires are *partial*). Separatist desires may also be *comprehensive*, in which case they're directed toward all religious aliens; or *noncomprehensive*, in which case they're directed only to some. Those who advocate *conversion* of religious aliens want to *domesticate* them, to make them into religious kin; they are *evangelists*, and their activity is *evangelical*. They may have *comprehensive* evangelical desires, in which case they want to evangelize everyone; or *noncomprehensive* ones, in which case they want to evangelize only some. Evangelical methods may favor *compulsion*, in which case evangelism is accompanied by threat; *persuasion*, in which case it is accompanied by argument; or *presentation*, in which case it relies simply upon being present to those whose conversion is hoped for.

Your *salvation* is your proper end, the fulfilment of your purpose. On the question of what belonging to a religion has to do with being saved, there are *pluralists*, who think that all religions are equally effective in bringing salvation about; *exclusivists*, who think that belonging to the home religion is necessary for salvation; and *inclusivists*, who think that while belonging to the home religion is advantageous for salvation, belonging to an alien religion may sometimes suffice. On the question of who gets saved, there are *restrictivists*, whose claim is that not all do; and *universalists*, whose claim is that all do.

# CHAPTER 1

# *Religious Diversity*

## 1.1 Religion: Some Historical Remarks

There is no general agreement about what the term *religion* means. It follows that there is also no general agreement about how to decide when some pattern of human activity or belief is religious, how many religions there are, or where one religion ends and another begins. Christians, Jews, Buddhists, Muslims, and Hindus (among others) sometimes call their forms of life religions and themselves religious people. When they do, they may have relatively precise ideas about what it is to be religious; but such ideas tend to be derived by generalization from what they believe and practice as Christians, Jews, Buddhists (or whatever the case may be), and not to be widely shared (or even understood) beyond those communities. People who do not think of themselves as religious are generally less likely than those who do to have given much thought to the question of what religion is; and even where they have, perhaps forced to do so by professional need (constitutional lawyers with First Amendment interests, for example, or historians concerned to understand Hindu/Muslim hatreds in post-independence India) the views they arrive at are likely to be of use only for narrowly technical purposes.

The upshot is that the term *religion* is like *art* or *pornography* in being very difficult for native speakers of English to reach consensus about. Some of us, like terriers with rats, know religion when we see it and have deep feelings roused by it, but are quite incapable of offering a definition. Others, like people deaf from birth with music, can't recognize it and have little interest in it. Yet others make a profession of writing about it and studying it, and yet are disinterested, like apolitical historians of politics or nonmusical musicologists.

There is much evidence of a lack of consensus about how to use the term religion and its derivatives. For native speakers of English at the end of the twentieth century, the adverb *religiously* often means something very much like *habitually* or *seriously*. We say that she follows the White Sox religiously, or that he reads the *New York Times* religiously. But in this sense almost anything can be done religiously. Neither does the adjective *religious* provide much more help. "They're very religious, you know," may mean that they frequently go to church, that they know the Qur'an well, believe that what the Pope says is true, derive beliefs about the proper uses of human sexuality from a study of the Bible, judge the political life of a nation in light of Confucian ideas about ritual, self-flagellate on Fridays, or are celibate. It's not easy to see a common denominator here, and perhaps still less easy to say what it is even when there seems to be one.

There's an almost equally wide variety of opinion among those charged with making legal or political decisions about what a religion is, or about which patterns of human activity are best called religious. Many nations have to decide whether some particular pattern of human association constitutes a religion. In the United States, religious institutions are exempt from certain forms of taxation, and religious practices are given some constitutional protection; in England, religious instruction is mandatory in state-financed schools; and in Indonesia, the state finds it useful to determine to which religion each of its citizens belongs, and to include that information on the identity cards that all must carry. Such situations require the state sometimes to decide whether some pattern of human activity and association is or is not religious, and it often proves very difficult for courts and other agents of the state to arrive at the necessary decisions. These difficulties are a direct result of a lack of clarity and consensus about what religion means.

Religion is not alone in being difficult in this way. Similar things could be said about poetry or politics, and of course about philosophy. Readers of a book about any of these topics are likely to benefit from some remarks about how the author understands the topic at hand if they are not to be forced to struggle through a pervasive and thick conceptual fog as they read. It is the chief task of this chapter to make some such remarks, and there is no better place to begin than with some remarks on the history of the term.

Augustine, thinking and writing in North Africa at the end of the fourth and the beginning of the fifth century, understood *religion* (composing in Latin, he used the term *religio*) to mean worship, those patterns of action by which people self-consciously turn themselves toward God in homage and praise.[1] There could, he thought, be right and proper ("true") ways of worshipping God, just as there could be improper and damnable ("false") ways of doing so. Since Augustine was a Catholic Christian, he also thought that Christian worship was, on the whole, identical with true religion, and that although true religion was not found only within the bounds of the Christian church, it was found pre-eminently and most perfectly there.

This equation of religion with worship was not unique to Augustine. It was almost standard in the pre-Christian Mediterranean world, and it became the ordinary understanding of *religio* among those Christians of late antiquity who thought and wrote in Latin. This understanding of the word is evident, too, in the etymology of *religio* most commonly given by Latin-using intellectuals (Christian and otherwise) in late antiquity. This etymology derives *religio* from *re* + *ligare*, "to bind back," or "to re-bind," meaning to re-establish by worship a lost or broken intimacy between God and worshippers. There is another etmyology, defended by a minority both ancient and modern, which derives *religio* from *re* + *legere*, "to re-read"; but this etymology has entered less deeply into the soul of the West.[2]

*Religio*, however, was not a word of great importance to the philosophers and theologians of late antiquity. Neither was it of much importance to Western Christians. This was in part because there is no significant biblical term (in Hebrew or Greek) naturally and consistently rendered by *religio* (in Latin) or *religion* (in English). The King James Version of the Bible (1611), for instance, uses *religion* or *religious* only five times in its rendering of the New Testament from Greek, and for three different Greek terms. Jerome's Latin version uses *religio* and its derivatives only six times, also to translate a number of different Greek words (and not always the same ones as those rendered with *religion* by the translators of the King James Version).

From the time of Jerome (fourth century) until the Renaissance (fifteenth century), Western Christians had little occasion to think or write about those things that we now usually call *religions*. Islam did not come into existence until the seventh century, and until the Renaissance was most often thought of by Christians as a Christian heresy rather than a non-Christian religion; the religions of India, China, Japan, Africa, and America were effectively unknown until the sixteenth century; and Judaism, in spite of the many lively Jewish communities in Europe, was a topic of interest to Christians largely as a precursor to Christianity, a preparation for the gospel. The result was that Christianity was rarely, if ever, thought of by Christians as one religion among many: Christians did not, before the modern period, have the idea that there is a type called *religion* of which there are many tokens or instances – Christianity, Hinduism, Islam, Confucianism, and so on (just as there is a type called *currency* of which there are many tokens – dollars, euros, pounds, deutschmarks, and so on). The idea that religion is a type with tokens is largely a modern invention.

Insofar as there was a standard use of the term *religion* in Europe between the effective end of Roman hegemony in the fifth century and the cataclysm of the Reformation in the sixteenth, it was to denote the activities and members of the monastic orders. These were typically called religious orders, and their members were simply the religious. This usage has survived, in somewhat attenuated form, in the Roman Catholic Church, where it is possible still to hear people speak of *the religious life* and mean by it life as a vowed member of a monastic order.

The modern (post-Reformation) understandings of religion differ from these premodern uses most dramatically in that they see religion exactly as a type of which there are many tokens. One influence upon the acceptance of this idea was the pressing necessity in the seventeenth century of creating political forms of life in Europe that could peacefully accommodate a wide variety of Christian groups with incompatible understandings of what it is to be a Christian, and often with a deep hatred of one another. After the Thirty Years' War in Europe (1618–48) and the Civil War in England (1642–8), in which such differences showed themselves clearly in large-scale and long-lived violence, it was clear that the political forms which had served Europe fairly well for the preceding millennium would no longer do, and that any new ones would have to find a way of dealing with the violent splintering of Christendom brought about by the Reformation.

The political solutions that emerged were of two kinds. The first affirmed the idea that a sovereign state could and should accommodate only one Christian group, and that your religion (now it began commonly to be called that) should therefore be determined by geography, by where you happened to live. Calvin's Geneva provides one instance of this solution, as does the English settlement of 1688; both use the idea that there are many religions, and that the state should establish and give special privileges to just one among them. The second kind of political resolution used the idea that the state should be neutral or even-handed with respect to religion (which usually meant neutral with respect to the various brands of Protestant Christianity; Jews and Catholics were usually beyond the pale, and Buddhists and Muslims did not even enter into consideration). The passage of the First Amendment to the American Constitution in 1791 provides an example here. This second kind of political resolution, like the first, required (usually in very explicit terms) the view that there are many religions.

But it was not only the division of Christianity into many different and often warring groups in the sixteenth and seventeenth centuries that contributed to the idea that religion is a type with many tokens. Almost equally important was the vast increase in European knowledge of the history, languages, and practices of non-European civilizations. Beginning in the fifteenth century (and increasing almost exponentially in the sixteenth and seventeenth), reports of the habits and practices of the Indians, the Chinese, the Japanese, and the inhabitants of Meso-America began to be available to the literati of Europe. The earliest among these reports were written by Catholic missionaries for the use of the church in its efforts to propagate itself; but these were soon followed by work sponsored by the European states with interests in empire-building – first the Portuguese, Spanish, and Dutch, and later the English and French. By the seventeenth century, grammars and lexica of hitherto exotic and unknown languages (Sanskrit, Chinese) began to become available, and throughout the eighteenth and nineteenth centuries works in these languages were translated in ever-increasing numbers into those of Europe.

Much of the information gathered in these ways seemed to European intellectuals to reveal forms of life and patterns of belief both deeply like and importantly unlike Christian forms and patterns. The Indians wrote hymns and prayers to many gods, and seemed to worship images and statues of them; the Chinese had temples, sacred works, and a highly developed ritual system; and so on. It began to seem natural to European historians, philosophers, and theologians to think of these forms of life as the religions of India and China, and also to think of Christianity as the religion of Europe. It was then not difficult to move to the more abstract theoretical view that there is a type called religion of which there are many tokens; and this was effectively the standard position by the eighteenth century, though with many deep disagreements about how best to understand what religion is, and how best to account for the variety of religions. These are disagreements with whose legacy we must still deal.

Parson Thwackum, a character in Henry Fielding's novel *Tom Jones*, first published in 1749, provides a good example of the type-token way of thinking about religion, and of the deep insularity and exclusivism which often accompanied it (Fielding treats Thwackum satirically, and does not here endorse his opinions):

> When I mention religion, I mean the Christian religion; and not only the Christian religion, but the Protestant religion; and not only the Protestant religion, but the Church of England.[3]

*Religion* thus became a term of art for European intellectuals, and one that proved endlessly fascinating, prompting the painting of many theoretical pictures. Some of these depicted a single ur-religion from which all others had descended (the Christian version of this tended to depict non-Christian religions originating in the linguistic chaos that followed the destruction of the Tower of Babel described in Genesis 11); others, like David Hume in his *Natural History of Religion* (1757), offered theories of religion according to which every token of the type could be accounted for by appeal solely to psychological and sociological variables, and so without any reference to God; yet others offered evolutionary views, according to which the variety of religions could be accounted for by such mysteries as the progressive self-revelation of spirit in history (Hegel's *Lectures on the Philosophy of Religion*, presenting an argument of this sort, were first given in 1821). And so on, into the twenty-first century.

This particular history is uniquely European, and the use of *religion* as a term of art is intimately, even symbiotically linked with it. It should therefore not be surprising that intellectuals uninfluenced by this history tend to lack a term of art anything like religion. Premodern Christians, as already indicated, were largely innocent of it; and it is on the whole true to say that non-Christians (except where they have been influenced by this same history) also lack it. Even if it's reasonable to judge that (say) both Buddhism and Christianity are tokens of the type *religion* (and on some understandings of religion it is no doubt reasonable so to judge), it does not follow from this that Buddhists naturally think (or should think) of Buddhism in this way. There is an indigenous Buddhist lexicon that will do some of the same work for them as *religion* does for us. But there is no close match and no reason to expect one. The desire to philosophize about religion and to think of religion as a type with tokens is very much a product of a particular European history.

One result of this peculiar European history and the intellectual work that has gone along with it is precisely the variegated and complex understanding of religion we now have. The desire for religious tolerance produced by the political pressures of early modernity has now been written into the constitutions of most democratic states, but usually without much consensus about what a religion is. The large amount of theoretical thought about the nature of religion and about the proper way to think of the relations among various tokens of the type has not led to any deep consensus among those who engage in it. And the range of uses given to *religion* in ordinary language is, as already indicated, very broad indeed and not capable of easy resolution into a coherent whole.

I'll give the novelist Walker Percy the last word on this matter: "a peculiar word this in the first place, *religion*; it is something to be suspicious of."[4]

## 1.2 Religion: A Definition

In this situation, what to do? This is, after all, a book on the philosophical questions raised by religious diversity. Are we condemned to not knowing what we are talking about? Fortunately not. The best solution in a situation like this is to offer a more or less stipulative understanding of religion, one that is somewhat responsive both to the history that has made it necessary for us to have some understanding of what we mean by *religion*, and to the meanings and uses currently given that term in intellectual and political life. Such a definition should also be such that it will serve the needs of the enterprise for which it is constructed; and since the enterprise here is an exploration of the philosophical problems raised by religious diversity, the stipulative definition offered should make it possible fruitfully to explore those questions. It is with these constraints and needs in mind that I offer the following definition of religion. It is not the only possible or single best definition; it is merely one that, while being (I hope) adequately responsive to the historical and lexical context mentioned, will be appropriate and useful for the topic of this book.

A religion, then, I shall take to be a form of life that seems to those who inhabit it to be comprehensive, incapable of abandonment, and of central importance. When I use *religion* or its derivatives (*religious, religiously*, and so on) in what follows, I shall have this understanding in mind. But it needs further clarification, and that is best provided by making a few comments about its constituent terms.

Let's begin by considering what a *form of life* is. This I shall take to be a pattern of activity that seems to those who belong to it to have boundaries and particular actions proper or intrinsic to it. For most married people, marriage is a form of life in this sense. It is bounded in the sense that there are patterns of activity and particular actions outside it, not intrinsic or proper to it, without which it can perfectly well continue to be what it is; there are also patterns of activity and particular actions intrinsic and proper to it, without which it cannot continue. The division between the former and the latter marks the boundary of the form of life called marriage (perhaps better, "being married") – or so it probably seems to many married people. When I teach a class at the university that pays my wages, I am (it seems to me) engaged in an action that is not intrinsic or proper to being married; it falls outside the boundary of that form of life, and this is true even though it may be related causally to being married (perhaps I am caused to do it in part to earn money to support the children who are the product of my marriage). By contrast, making love with my wife, sharing a bed with her and living with her and our children, talking with her about our children's peccadilloes and possible futures – all these are (it seems to me) activities proper to the form of life that is marriage: they fall within its bounds.

Another example: I play squash, and this (it seems to me) is a form of life, even though rather a circumscribed one. There are particular actions proper and intrinsic to it (hitting the ball), there are its hallowed places (the court, the locker room), its sacred implements (the racket and ball), and its appropriate dress. The patterns of activity closely associated with these places and things fall within the game of squash; those not so connected (the vast majority of the things I do) fall outside its boundaries.

There are no natural or inevitable ways to individuate forms of life. There will always be many (perhaps infinitely many) possible ways of cutting the cake. I might, for example, want to connect my playing of squash with my occasional workouts in the gym and my occasional bicycle rides with my son, and say that they all belong to the form of life called *taking physical exercise*. It might seem to me that this is the natural thing to do if I'm questioned by my doctor about how much exercise I take. At other times and in other situations I might want to think of playing squash and riding a bicycle as separate forms of life. In spite of this fluidity in our drawing of lines between one form of life and another, it remains true that most of us most of the time work with a fairly stable understanding of how many forms of life we inhabit and where their boundaries are; and that many of us could, if pressed, say a good deal about what these are and about the actions proper to each. In my own case, the first few forms of life that come to mind are being a Christian, being a husband, being a father, and being a writer.

Recall that according to my definition religion is a form of life in the sense given, but one with three particular defining characteristics: it seems to those who belong to it to be *comprehensive, incapable of abandonment,* and *of central importance.* A word now about each of these.

First, *comprehensiveness.* If a form of life seems to those who belong to it to be comprehensive, then it seems to them to take account of and be relevant to everything – not only to the particulars of all the forms of life they live in, but to everything in the strict sense. How can this be? For example: a Brahmin (a high-caste Hindu) who attempts seriously to live as such might see his Brahminism as providing a frame for all the other forms of life he belong to. If he is married, he will understand the fact of his marriage, together with all the particular activities that constitute it, as in large part prescribed by (and in every particular framed by) the theoretical perspectives on marriage enshrined in the relevant ethico-legal injunctions found in the texts and traditions that are authoritative for Brahmins. The same will be true for his mode of dress, the physical posture he adopts while defecating, and what he does to make a living. There will be no form of life and no particular action or pattern of action that fails to seem to him to be a proper part of his Brahminism. And not only this: the form of life which is orthoprax Brahminism will (or may) seem to those who belong to it to provide an account of absolutely everything – of the nature of the physical universe, of the mathematical disciplines, of the languages and cultural habits of *mlecchas* (non-Indians) – and so on.

It is of course not the case that our serious Brahmin will find that his Brahminism provides him with the truth about the particulars of all these matters. His form of life will probably not give him knowledge of whether Goldbach's Conjecture (that every even number greater than two can be expressed as the sum of two primes) is true (nobody knows), or accurate information as to the etymology of the English word *juggernaut* (it comes from a Sanskrit compound meaning *protector of the universe*). But because his Brahminism is (or seems to him to be) a comprehensive form of life, it will provide him with the frame into which matters of this sort can be placed, and with a particular place in this frame so that he can tell what kind of issue each is. Questions in number theory like the truth of Goldbach's Conjecture might be thought of as having their answers contained (by implication) in the *Veda* (the fundamental authoritative text for Brahmins), even if the particular answer is not known; and questions in English etymology might be included under the category of matters having to do with barbarian languages, about which good

Brahmins neither know nor need to know any particulars. The point in every case will be that those who take themselves to belong to a comprehensive form of life, nothing falls outside or is irrelevant to that frame. Everything is comprised within it and given a particular location therein.

There is perhaps a trivial sense in which every form of life is comprehensive. After all, every such form, even very limited ones like playing squash, locates every other form of life as either being within itself or not being within itself. The squash player may then take account of forms of life such as teaching or being married under the general description *forms of life that have nothing directly to do with playing squash*. But this is a different kind of comprehensiveness than that found in our Brahminical example. The former might be called comprehensiveness-by-exclusion and the latter comprehensiveness-by-inclusion; only the latter is characteristic of religious forms of life. Such forms do not sit alongside others, excluding some as other than or irrelevant to themselves. Instead, they englobe or contain these others, providing a frame within which they have their being and meaning. If a circle represents a form of life, then most of us will seem to ourselves to inhabit many circles. But those of us who seem to ourselves to inhabit a religiously comprehensive form of life will find that all the many small circles are contained within one large one, the circle that represents our religion.

However, not all comprehensive forms of life are best thought of as religious. Any particular comprehensive form of life should, if it is so to be thought of, also seem to those who inhabit it to be *incapable of abandonment* and *of central importance*. Some comments now on each of these.

For a comprehensive form of life to seem to those who belong to it incapable of abandonment it must seem to them that living in it is sufficiently constitutive or definitive of who they are that leaving it is impossible without also leaving themselves. All of us, I expect, belong to forms of life that seem to us like this. The most obvious example for is the form of life constituted by speaking and thinking in our native language. I live in the house of English in this way, and it seems to me that I can't cease to do so. This doesn't mean, of course, that I can't learn to read or speak another language; but it does mean that in so learning I will always and necessarily be a native speaker of English grafting another linguistic skill upon the trunk of my Englishness. Abandoning the form of life *speaking English natively* is certainly unimaginable to me, even if not strictly inconceivable.

A religious form of life will also be like this. It will seem to those who inhabit it not only to be comprehensive, but also to be incapable of abandonment. A Catholic Christian, for example, baptized as a baby, trained up in the faith, a regular and faithful attender at Mass, a reader of the Bible, a sayer of prayers – such a person is likely to be in the same case as a native speaker of English. She may be able to express in words the claim that she might cease to be a native speaker of English. But such expressions will be as imaginatively empty as the claim *I might run a mile in two minutes* or *I might be able to solve cube roots in my head with rapidity and ease*. They will bear no phenomenal content, which is to say that they will conjure nothing but a concept in the minds of those who use them.

Yet a third characteristic needs to be added to comprehensiveness and incapability of abandonment in order to make a form of life religious. It is *centrality*. To say of a form of life that it is central for those who belong to it is to say that it seems to them to address the questions of paramount importance to the ordering of their lives. Such a question might be: Should I think about and behave toward all humans as if they were in all important respects equal? A Catholic Christian form of life will provide an affirmative answer to this question (all humans have been created by God and bear God's image, and as a result should be so treated); a Brahminical Hindu one will provide a negative answer (your fundamental duties toward any particular human being are given by your respective places in the ordered hierarchy of caste; this will differ from case to case). Other such questions might be: How should I understand my fundamental purpose in life? Should I kill and eat sentient nonhuman creatures? Is beauty the primary value? And so on.

There is no single set of questions that will seem of paramount importance to everyone. A question of paramount importance to one may be an irrelevance or an annoyance to another, though it is likely that there will be a relatively small number of questions that seem of paramount importance to people – most humans are concerned, it seems, about purpose, meaning, the significance of death, how to avoid pain, and so on. But the fact that there is no single set of questions that will seem of paramount importance to everyone for the ordering of their lives indicates an important fact about the account of religious forms of life given in this book. It is an account in terms of how the forms of life that people belong to *seem to them*, not one in terms of how those forms of life actually are. Approaching the matter in this way has a number of advantages. The most obvious is that it avoids the difficulty of specifying what the content of a religious form of life should be, a matter that has proved notoriously difficult. Should religious forms of life have to do with God, the gods, or other supernatural beings? Should they specify ethical codes or patterns of ritual observance? Should they involve views about the life (or lives) that follow upon physical death? On the understanding of what makes a form of life religious given here, any or all of these things might belong to such forms of life, but none need do so. Everything will depend upon how a form of life appears to those who belong to it.

In summary: For the purposes of the investigations to be carried out in this book, a religion will be understood as a form of life that seems to those who belong to it to be comprehensive, incapable of abandonment, and of central importance to the ordering of their lives. It is the great circle that seems to religious people to contain all the small circles representing their noncomprehensive forms of life; it is a form of life the abandonment of which seems to those who inhabit it to be tantamount to the abandonment of their identity; and it is a form of life that permits address to the questions that seem to those who belong to it to matter more than any others.

## 1.3   Diversity in Religion

On this understanding of religion, what is to be said about religious diversity? The first and obvious point is that there are likely to be many religions, which is to say that there are likely to be many different forms of life that seem to those who belong to them to be comprehensive, incapable of abandonment, and of central importance. This can reasonably be said without knowledge of the particulars of any such forms of life. It is, after all, easily possible to imagine religions significantly different from one another in their particulars. A man excessively devoted to his wife might, for instance, live in his marriage as a form of life of the relevant sort; in such a case, *being married* would seem to him to comprehend all his other forms of life, to be constitutive of his very being, and to address all questions of central importance to his life. Another person, excessively committed politically, might belong to a form of life in which the party (whatever it happens to be) provides a comprehensive form of life that seems incapable of abandonment, and so forth. Perhaps such people are in important respects pathological or deluded; but there can be no doubt that the forms of life they belong to are religious in the sense in play here.

This imagination of religious diversity shows only that significantly different religions may exist. But even the most superficial investigation of particular forms of life that seem, on the face of things, to qualify as religious makes this possiblity actual: not only can there be significantly different religions, but there actually are. The particulars of a Marxist form of life that seems to its inhabitants comprehensive, incapable of abandonment, and centrally important (and there are still Marxists who inhabit Marxism religiously) are deeply different from the particulars of a Christian form of life that bears the same characteristics for those who belong to it. And the same would have to be said, with appropriate changes of substance, for the particulars of a Buddhist form of life as compared with those of an Islamic form of life. And so on. This fact, the fact that there is deep religious diversity, raises two questions immediately. First, what makes one religion different from another? Second, how does the kind of difference among religions so far mentioned map on to the great complexes of thought and practice often called the *world religions* – Christianity, Buddhism, Islam, and so on?

It's relatively easy to answer the first question – What makes one religion different from another? – in a formal way. A religion ceases to be the religion it is just when one or more of the elements essential to it is lost by abandonment or transformation; and one religion is different from another just when it is not possible for the same person to inhabit both at the same time. For example, it may seem to those who inhabit a Buddhist form of life that loss of any contact with members of the Sangha, the monastic order, is also loss of something essential to their religion, and as a result amounts to the abandonment of it. Or, it may seem to a Muslim who adds belief in the Trinity to his Islamic form of life that he has replaced it thereby with a new one because the theism that informed the old religion has been transformed. By contrast, it may seem to a Reform Jew who becomes Orthodox that she has not abandoned or replaced her earlier religious form of life, but only modified it as one might modify one's marriage by adding to it a severer and more demanding observance of the disciplines of love. And, finally, it seems reasonable to say that Greek Orthodox Christianity and Gelug Tibetan Buddhism are different religions just because it is performatively impossible to belong to both at once – in much the same way that it's performatively impossible simultaneously to be a sumo wrestler and a balance-beam gymnast, or natively to live in the house of English and the house of Japanese.

But this formal way of answering the question is not very helpful because it at once raises new and equally difficult questions about which elements of a religion are essential to it and which are not. These questions are not capable of any single answer that all (or even most) will agree with. Forms of life (religious or other) do not group themselves into categories neatly, any more than do forms of plant or animal life. It is of course possible to state criteria by which to decide whether two trees are members of the same species, just as it is possible to state criteria by which to decide whether two forms of religious life belong to the same species. It might, for instance, be said that all religions for which belief in and worship of a single, omnipotent, omniscient God appears to be of central importance belong to the species *theistic religion*; it might also be said that all members of this species that make use of the Qur'an belong to the subspecies *Islamic theistic religion*. Or, it would be possible to say that all forms of religious life that give great importance to the celebration of large-scale public rituals belong to a single species. Perhaps Communism in some of its forms (think of the May Day parades) would belong in this species, as might some forms of Hinduism (think of the parades of statues of gods through city streets in India on festival days).

There will, then, always be many (perhaps infinitely many) ways to sort religions into kinds, just as is true for sorting plants or animals. But this doesn't mean that all ways of doing so are equally good. Rather, any particular way of doing it will be at the service of an interest or purpose of the sorter, and will be good or bad to the extent that it serves that purpose. One popular way of sorting religions (sufficiently popular and sufficiently familiar that it will have to be used a good deal in this book) is by a complex mixture of historical connection, geographic contiguity, and observable features. This is how we get *Christian* as a sortal term used to place together those religions related causally in some more or less direct way to the life, death, and resurrection of Jesus of Nazareth, and that bear some common features of practice, such as baptism and eucharist (though choosing which features are essential to Christianity is a matter of deep controversy among Christians). And, similarly, this is how we get *Hindu* as a sortal term used to place together those religions that originated in India or in some part of the sphere of Indian cultural influence, and that are not Buddhist, Sikh, or Jain. This way of sorting religions gives us what are typically called the *world religions*, listed and explained in the textbooks of religion used in Western schools and colleges. Like Linnaeus's sorting and ordering of forms of plant life, this taxonomy has both a complex history and many uses; but it is obviously not the only way to cut the cake.

A more technical way to put the points made in the last few paragraphs is to say that where religions are concerned there are no obvious natural kinds. A natural kind is a category (class, species, type) whose boundaries are given by the order of the cosmos itself, and which any taxonomic act adequate to its task ought therefore to recognize. It is a moot point whether there are any natural kinds; it is even more moot whether, if there are, we humans are in a position to recognize them and to say with clarity, certainty, and cogency what their boundaries are and what characteristics something ought to possess in order to belong to one or another of them. But this is a subject I won't pursue further here. I'll assume in what follows that if there are natural kinds among religions we are not in a position to be able to reach general agreement about what they are and where their boundaries lie; and that we ought therefore to think of any particular sorting of religions into kinds (at least any intended for a wide audience, one that does not share convictions that would, if shared, make some particular sorting of religions seem natural or obvious) as a useful fiction. I shall often write of *Christian* or *Buddhist* or *Islamic* forms of life in this book; but it's important to keep in mind that I shall always be so understanding the acts of classification that inform such locutions.

It's also worth emphasizing what should already be obvious: religious forms of life as understood in this book are not to be found only within the so-called world religions; neither are all the forms of life found there properly religious. It is perfectly possible (if a bit odd) for someone to have a religious form of life whose central object is a sports team (the true fan), a particular form of intellectual work (the true scientist), or another person (the true lover). These are religious forms of life that do not easily find a place within the bounds of one of the world religions. Similarly, many who adopt a form of life that does belong to one of the world religions does not thereby always adopt (what I am calling) a religion. For instance, a liberal Reform Jew in England might well say that he is Jewish in response to a question on a census form; but he might also treat his Jewishness as a matter of marginal importance to his life as a whole (as something functionally similar to his habit of playing golf on a Sunday, perhaps). And insofar as he does this, his Jewishness is not, for him, a comprehensively central form of life that seems incapable of abandonment.

A further point. The religious forms of life collected together by the sortal terms *Christian*, *Jewish*, and so forth, will often be extraordinarily varied, and may, on some other principles of sorting, not seem to belong together at all. The features common to a form of life inhabited by a member of the Gush Emmunim in Israel and that lived in by a Hasidic Jew in New Jersey are few, and those that differentiate them many. The same is true for the features common to a form of life belonged to by a Theravada Buddhist in a forest hermitage in Sri Lanka and that belonged to by a Friend of the Western Buddhist Order in England: each is nominally Buddhist, but the features that differentiate them are perhaps more numerous (and on some accounts more significant) than those they share.

To recapitulate these remarks on diversity in religion. The point of significance for this book is that religious diversity is real. There is a wide variety of religious forms of life, and at least on the surface these differ deeply among themselves, most obviously in what they take to be of central importance and in the patterns of action that inform and order them. Such surface differences may be compatible with some kind of deeper unity; this is a point to be addressed in later chapters, as also is the question of what kinds of differences there are among religious forms of life, and the question of how deep they go.

## 1.4  Philosophical Questions about Religious Diversity

If it's difficult to say what a religion is, it's at least as difficult to say what philosophy is, and so also what a philosophical question is. Certainly there is no widespread agreement among professional philosophers about the scope and method of their discipline, and I shall not try to do better than they. I shall simply note three questions suggested by the fact of religious diversity, questions whose discussion prompts reasoned argument and rational discussion among philosophers.

But who is a philosopher? Etymology says that philosophers are lovers of wisdom; Plato that philosophy is a training for death;[5] and John Locke that philosophers are underlabourers in the service of science.[6] But I shall mean nothing so exalted or so complicated. Instead, I shall take philosophical work to be centrally concerned with analysis of claims and arguments, and those who do such work to be philosophers (at least while they're doing it). On this understanding, when faced with a particular claim, philosophers will typically ask what it means, whether it might be true, and whether anyone ought to believe it. Asking these things often leads them to ask what meaning is, how truth might be understood, and whether belief is a useful category. And this taste for abstraction on the part of philosophers leads them to be interested precisely in the kinds of questions that permit or even encourage the indulgence of such tastes. This will be evident in the questions I shall identify as of interest to philosophers in connection with religious diversity.

The first of my three questions has truth as its central topic. There are many religions; they all seem to require of those who belong to them assent to or acceptance of some claims about the way things are; these claims frequently are (or seem to be) incompatible one with another. These facts have led to considerable argument (much of it reasoned and reasonable) and a good deal of reflection (of which at least some is rational) among philosophers. Suppose we call a claim assent to or acceptance of which is required (or very strongly recommended) by inhabiting some particular form of religious life a *religious claim*. The fact of religious diversity then suggests the following question: Given the fact of religious diversity, what can reasonably be said about the truth of religious claims? This question, together with its penumbra of associated and derived questions, will be the central topic of chapter 2. Notice that this is not a question about the truth of particular religious claims considered by themselves – claims like *the Buddha is the best of all humans*, or *all things were made by God*, or *support of the White Sox is the highest human good*. Argument about the truth of such claims may arise quite independently of religious diversity. Instead, the central question of chapter 2 has to do with what may be said about the truth of such claims in general, considered in the light (or perhaps the obscurity) of religious diversity.

The second of my three questions has to do with epistemic confidence, confidence that an act of assent to a claim does indeed bring you knowledge, or ought to be made, or has been formed in the right way, the way that such assents ought to be formed. (Deciding among these various ways of putting what epistemic confidence is requires decisions about some delicate matters in epistemology, or theory of knowledge; some of these matters will be touched on when this second question comes to be discussed in chapter 3.)

Some of your acts of assent to particular claims are made with a good deal of epistemic confidence – perhaps your assent to the claim *the sun will rise tomorrow* is like this; others are made with a good deal less – perhaps your assent to the claim *more people live in London than in New York* is like this. Coming to know of diversity in religious belief raises some questions about the epistemic confidence with which religious assents are and should be made, and it is these questions that will be the central topic of chapter 3. In its most general and abstract form, the question of chapter 3 is: Does (or should) coming to know of religious diversity reduce or remove religious people's epistemic confidence in the religious assents they find themselves making?

My third question has to do with the religious alien. A religious alien is one who belongs to a form of religious life other than your own. It follows from such a definition that one person's religious alien is another person's religious kin. If you belong to a particular religion, then all those who belong to a different one (bearing in mind the difficulties already mentioned involved in saying where one religion ends and another begins) will be religious aliens so far as you are concerned. And if you belong to no religious form of life, then all those who do are religious aliens so far as you are concerned. The fact of religious diversity establishes directly that there are religious aliens, and this in turn raises a question of philosophical interest, one to which reasoned argument can be directed. This is, in its most general form: What attitudes toward the religious alien are possible? Closely connected with this is the question of how the religious alien ought to be treated. These are questions likely to be approached somewhat differently by those who belong to a form of religious life than by those who do not. Chapter 4 will be devoted to an exploration of the responses that may be given to this question, and to the advantages and disadvantages of each.

Chapter 5 will treat a particular issue that combines elements of those treated in the second, third, and fourth chapters. It is a question of especially pressing concern to many of those who are religious, and usually of correspondingly less concern for those who are not. It is the question of salvation, to use a Christian word for it, and it may be formulated in this way: How may humans realize their proper end? Those who belong to most religious forms of life think that there is such an end, that it is the one prescribed by the form of life they live in, and that the very same form of life makes its attainment possible. Christians, for example, might think that the end in question is the love and service of God here below, and, after the resurrection of the body, the beatific vision. Buddhists might think that it is the attainment of Nirvana, which is the end of the cycle of redeath and rebirth together with the suffering that accompanies that cycle. Those who belong to no religious form of life are less likely to think that there is such an end, although it is by no means impossible that they should. The purpose of the discussion in chapter 5 is not finally to resolve this question to the satisfaction of all (though that would be a fine windmill to tilt at), but rather, as with the other chapters, to explore how religious diversity does (or should) affect answers to it.

These questions, I take it, are the central questions of philosophical interest raised by religious diversity. They are certainly those to which most discussion has been given by philosophers in recent years, and my analysis will attempt to provide something of a guide to the current debate, as well as to argue for particular solutions to at least some of them.

## 1.5   Standpoints and Answers

What has been said to this point should already have made it apparent that the questions raised or sharpened by religious diversity will often look very different when viewed from inside a religious form of life than they will when viewed from outside. Likewise, answers to them that prove satisfactory to someone who is religious will very likely not so prove to someone who is not. This is perhaps most obvious in connection with the question of how to treat the religious alien. This will have to be approached very differently by the nonreligious than by the religious, for the former will likely feel pressed to make decisions about it that apply indifferently to all religious people (since all religious people are alien to them), while the latter will not, since for them there will be at least one group of religious people (their coreligionists, their religious kin) who are not alien.

But the differences are present and urgent also in the case of the questions about truth and warrant that are the topic of the second and third chapters. For those who belong to a religious form of life there will typically be at least one set of religious claims that seem true and one set of religious assents that seem strongly warranted: those of the religion they belong to, the home religion. And this will of course typically not be the case for those who belong to no religion. It will be important to keep this difference of standpoint in mind; I shall sometimes be explicit in mentioning it, but even when I am not it will enter quite deeply into what I do say.

There are some religions with a long history of knowledge of and thought about religious diversity. It is important to keep in mind that such knowledge and thought is not, as some philosophers and theologians writing about it at the end of the twentieth century too often suggest, a peculiarly modern phenomenon. Indian religions, for example, have a very long history of developing responses to religious diversity; and Christianity was formed in the Mediterranean world at a time when thought about these matters was unavoidable. But other religions, by contrast, have little history of such knowledge, or have found it of relatively little importance to their self-understanding. In cases where there is a history of response to religious diversity it seems not unreasonable to suppose that there is some wisdom to be found in it (though always, of course, religion-specific wisdom), and I shall draw upon it in what follows.

There is also, now, a fairly long history of response to the philosophical problems raised by religious diversity on the part of those who belong to no religious form of life (or who are forced by the office they hold or the public functions they have to pretend they do not). This kind of response is found in writings by some avowedly secular philosophers, sociologists, and jurists. But it is found most fully (and in some respects most interestingly) in the body of judicial opinion connected with United States court decisions about cases that have to do with religious freedom. This is not to say that there is no comparable body of judicial opinion interpreting constitutional law to be found in other countries. But the United States Constitution provides in the so-called establishment clauses of the First Amendment ("Congress shall make no law respecting an establishment of religion, or prohibiting the free exercise thereof") an elegantly sharp statement as to the desirability of the state's not belonging to any particular form of religious life, and neither supporting nor opposing any by state action; and the other countries with constitutions of like kind (and corresponding bodies of judicial opinion) have mostly taken the United States version as their model. It therefore seems not unreasonable to draw upon United States judicial opinion (and especially Supreme Court opinion) upon relevant cases, and to assume that here too there is wisdom to be found upon the matters of concern to this book.

## NOTES

1   Augustine, *De vera religione* [True Religion], i.1–vi.11, trans. J. H. S. Burleigh in *Augustine: Earlier Writings* (Philadelphia: Westminster Press, 1953), pp. 225–83, at pp. 225–32; *De civitate dei* [City of God], x.1, trans. Henry Bettenson, *Concerning the City of God against the Pagans* (London: Pelican Books, 1972), pp. 371–4.

2   On the etymology and use of *religio* and *religion* see René Gothóni, "Religio and Superstitio Reconsidered," *Archiv für Religionspsychologie* 21 (1994), pp. 37–46. See also Jonathan Z. Smith, "Religion, Religions, Religious," in Mark C. Taylor, ed., *Critical Terms for Religious Studies* (Chicago: University of Chicago Press, 1998), pp. 269–84.

3   Henry Fielding, *The History of Tom Jones, A Foundling*, ed. Douglas Brooks-Davies (London: Dent, 1998; first published 1749), bk. 3, ch. 3, p. 98.

4   Walker Percy, *The Moviegoer* (New York: Pantheon, 1998; first published 1961), p. 237.

5   Plato, *Phaedo*, 67e. In Edith Hamilton and Huntington Cairns, ed., *The Collected Dialogues of Plato* (Princeton: Princeton University Press, 1963), p. 50.

6   John Locke, *Essay Concerning Human Understanding*, ed. Peter H. Nidditch (Oxford: Clarendon Press, 1975; first published 1690), p. 10.

# CHAPTER 2

# *Religious Diversity and Truth*

## 2.1 Religious Claims: Doctrines and Teachings

A religious claim, according to the definition already given, is a claim about the way things are, acceptance of or assent to which is required or strongly suggested by the fact of belonging to a particular form of religious life. I'll now say more about what is meant by this, provide some instances of religious claims, and make some suggestions about the importance that assent to or acceptance of them might have for being religious. These preliminaries are important because this chapter is concerned with the question of truth in the light of religious diversity, and (it will be argued) it is precisely religious claims that are potentially possessors of the interesting property *being true*. Some further understanding of what a religious claim is will therefore be useful.

What, then, is a claim about the way things are? Following (in part) the work of the philosopher William Christian,[1] I divide these into three kinds: claims about the setting of human life; claims about the nature of persons; and claims about the proper conduct of human life. This (perhaps like all categorizations) is a division made for convenience; it is not the only possible or single best division, but it will serve the purposes of this book well.

A claim about the setting of human life is, most typically, a descriptive claim about the environment in which we find ourselves and live our lives. Such a claim might be of very broad scope (*the world is the theater of God's glory*), or it might be very particular (*here is the Buddha's tooth*), but in all cases such claims will pick out some feature of the setting of human life (or perhaps the entirety of that setting) and will say that it is of a certain sort. It seems obvious on the face of things that if you belong to a religious form of life doing so will suggest to you (or require of you) assent to or acceptance of some claims of this sort. Suppose you are a religious Marxist. You are then likely to accept or assent to some version of the claim *epistemological opinions are always epiphenomena of economic arrangements*. If you're an Orthodox Jew you will be likely to accept or assent to some version of the claim *the Torah is of unparalleled significance as a revelation of what God intends for humans* – and so on.

A claim about the nature of humans is also typically a descriptive one, only this time one whose topic is not the setting of human life, but rather the nature of one of its kinds of inhabitants, or at least of some among those inhabitants. Again, it is obvious on the face of things that religions require (or strongly suggest) the making of some such claims on the part of their inhabitants. Instances might be: *a particular group of people has been given special duties by God*; *a particular group of people has been set aside as a field of great merit*; *all human hearts are restless until they find their rest in God*; and *people in a capitalist economic order are motivated principally by fear and greed*. I won't say more about what these claims might mean, nor about which religions might suggest them (though that ought to be fairly obvious). The only use of these claims here is as examples of claims about the nature of humans – the second kind of claim that religions will typically suggest to those who belong to them.

A claim about the proper conduct of human life (the third kind of claim) is typically put in the subjunctive or imperative mood, and requires, recommends, or suggests some pattern of action. And again, it is obvious at first blush that religions typically make some such claims upon those who belong to them. Instances might be: *Muslims ought to make pilgrimage to Mecca once in their lives*; *everyone ought to become a Christian*; *regular reading of the Bible is incumbent upon all Christians*; *all ought to bow the knee to Jesus*. The religious location of these four examples is explicit. Further examples might be taken from the moral codes contained in virtually all religions: the ten commandments, theoretically incumbent upon all Jews and Christians; the five precepts, theoretically incumbent upon all Buddhists – and so forth.

It is beyond doubt that many religions (recall that *religion* here is being understood to mean a form of life that seems to those who belong to it to be comprehensive, incapable of abandonment, and of central importance) are such that they have, over time, codified and ordered the claims (of all three mentioned kinds) that seemed to them to be required or suggested by belonging to that religion. In coming to belong to a religion of this sort you will typically make use of some such ready-to-hand codifications (Christians have their creeds, Buddhists their formulae, and so on), and will as a result easily be able to be explicit about the claims your religion requires of you. If you ask Catholic Christians what they believe about the setting of human life they may respond with parts of the Nicene Creed or the Baltimore Catechism (depending on their generation); and if you ask a Buddhist monk what he believes about the same matter, he may respond with the Four Truths or the twelvefold formulation of the chain of dependent co-origination.

But not all religions have found it necessary to produce such codifications; and even those that have do not codify in explicit form all the claims required of or suggested to those who belong to them. It is perfectly possible, therefore, for a religious person not to be able explicitly to state many of the claims to which her religion implicitly commits her. This is a familiar but important feature of human cognitive life. There are many claims, for example, about my wife to which I would assent were they propounded to me or were I to think of them, but which have never in fact been so propounded or which I have never in fact thought of, and to which therefore I have never given explicit assent. For instance, it was not until I was casting about for an instance of such a claim that I thought of the following: *my wife was not born in India.* Having thought of it I (involuntarily) assented to it. Just now, as I think of it, it is one of the explicit claims to which my assent is constrained by my being married to the woman to whom I am married. A few minutes ago it was one among the much larger sets of implicit claims to which my assent was constrained in the same way (and because of its deeply uninteresting nature I hope and expect that it will soon regain that status).

Particular religious people – even those who seem to themselves to share a religion – will vary enormously in the proportions of explicit to implicit claims to which they give their assent or acceptance. Such variations may be produced by temperament or accident. And, as already indicated, religions may vary among themselves in the extent to which they give explicit formulation to the claims of importance to them. But whatever the proportion of explicit to implicit claims, it will always be true that assent to or acceptance of more claims than those that are or (in practice) could be explicitly stated will be implied by belonging to a religious form of life. It is a legitimate and important part of the philosophy of religion to make explicit some of what is usually left implicit.

Questions remain, however. Are there, or could there be, religions that suggest to or require of those who belong to them no acts of assent? Are there, that is, forms of religious life that make no claims, explicitly or implicitly? It is fairly clear that there are not and cannot be. Imagine a religion that prescribes just one action for its adherents: if they sneeze when putting their shoes on in the morning they must at once go back to bed.[2] For this to qualify as a religion in the sense in play in this book, it will also be necessary to imagine (though it will be difficult to manage this) that those who belong to it find this prescription to constitute a form of life that is comprehensive, incapable of abandonment, and utterly central to their lives. Those who did so understand the prescription would, perhaps, scarcely be human; they would certainly be profoundly idiosyncratic. But even in the case of such an attenuated religion there is at least one explicit claim required (the prescription mentioned), together with a broad penumbra of claims implied, presupposed, and suggested by that one. And this is clearly true to a much greater extent of any decently well developed religion: those who live in the house of Judaism or Islam, for example, have an enormous number of claims, explicit and implicit, required of and/or suggested to them. All religions, therefore, require of and/or suggest to those who belong to them many acts of assent and acceptance. This will be assumed in what follows.

None of this is to say that claims are of equal importance to all religions (some may minimize the claims they require of or suggest to those who belong to them), or that all the claims of a particular religion are of equal importance to it. On this latter point: I've been saying that religions typically both suggest claims to those who belong to them and require claims of them. This distinction is meant to point to a difference in the degree of significance a claim may have for a religion. If assent to or acceptance of a claim is required by belonging to a religion, then the claim in question is central to that religion; this is to say that you can't belong to the religion without assenting to it. Such claims form the core, the heart, the umbra of that religion's claims.

More technically, when claims of this sort become explicit they are the religion's *doctrines*, those claims to which assent or acceptance is required of all who do or would like to belong to it. By contrast, if assent to or acceptance of a claim is suggested by belonging to a religion, then the claim in question is peripheral to that religion: you can belong to it without assenting to or accepting it. Such claims are at the periphery or are in the penumbra of that religion's claims. When such peripheral claims become explicit, they are the religion's *teachings*, those claims suggested by it but not required by it.

An example. It may seem to many Catholic Christians that the religious claim *Jesus is the Christ* (a claim about the setting of human life) is a doctrine of their religion, while the claim *frequently make private confes-*

*sion of your sins* (a claim about the proper conduct of human life) is a teaching. This is to say that refusing assent to or acceptance of *Jesus is the Christ* is tantamount to ceasing to be a Catholic Christian, while refusing assent to or acceptance of *frequently make private confession of your sins* is not. Other Catholic Christians may disagree, of course (and I intend no claim about the correct reading of Catholic Christianity on these matters); that this is so indicates the difficulty of coming to clear decisions about whether a particular claim is a doctrine or a teaching for those who belong to a particular religion. The distinction is important to bear in mind in spite of this difficulty, though, for it indicates a division very frequently made explicitly by those who belong to actual religions, as well as (usually in different terms) by those who belong to other forms of life.

Even in marriage, for instance, there are claims with doctrinal force and those with the force only of teachings; if I refuse assent to or acceptance of the claim *I intend faithfulness to and love of my spouse* I am thereby refusing a doctrine proper to marriage, and as a result leaving behind the form of life *being married*. But if I refuse assent to or acceptance of the claim *I must send my spouse red roses on St. Valentine's Day*, I am thereby refusing (at most) only one of the teachings proper to marriage. (No doubt there are different views of marriage than the one suggested by this distinction; but my interest here does not lie in making decisions about how marriage ought to be regarded.) In most of what follows I shall be interested in questions that have to do with the truth of religious doctrines rather than with that of religious teachings.

All religions have both doctrines and teachings (whether implicit or explicit), but not all need place the same importance upon them. Some may give primary importance to ritual action (to the proper worship of God, say; or to the correct mode of sacrificing a horse; or to the preferred way of serving the dictator), or to ethical action (to the love and service of neighbor, or to the support of the monastic order). I do not mean to give the impression that being religious frequently seems to those who are religious primarily to be a matter of assent to or acceptance of doctrines or teachings. This is certainly not the case for the Catholic Christian form of life with which I am most familiar – and this in spite of that religion's interest in formulating and codifying its doctrines and teachings. It is important to emphasize this as a check to those who would make of being religious primarily a form of intellectual life, which is to identify religious people primarily as believers. But it is equally important to emphasize, against those who would altogether remove the religious importance of acts of assent and acceptance, that all religions both do and must have doctrines and teachings, and that assent to or acceptance of these often seems of deep and desperate import to religious people.

## 2.2   Assent and Acceptance

A further distinction needs now to be made: that between assenting to a claim (whether a doctrine or a teaching), and accepting a claim. I've mentioned this distinction already, but it now needs to be explained. If you assent to a claim you take it to be true and to make a claim upon you; this is to say, roughly, that you believe it. Assenting to a claim in this sense is, by and large, an involuntary matter. As Lord Warburton puts it (in Henry James's *Portrait of a Lady*) to Isabelle Archer when she rejects his courtship, "If I could believe it, of course I should let you alone. But we can't believe by willing it . . ."[3] Warburton cannot believe that it would be better for him and for Isabelle that he should cease courting her. It is not, he thinks, within his power to give assent to this claim, and this is typical of all our acts of assent. If someone proposes to me the claim *Henry James is a better writer than P. G. Wodehouse* I find myself assenting to (believing) this claim; if I look out of the window on a sunny morning I find myself assenting to the claim *it's sunny out just now*. I assent to most of the teachings of my religion in the same way – claims such as *Jesus rose from the dead*, *God is triune*, and *I have a duty to attend Mass at least weekly*. In each case there is a long (and usually complicated) story to be told about why I find myself involuntarily moved to assent to these claims at a particular time. Usually, that story will involve reference to habits, skills, and knowledge I've gained in the past, but in all cases the upshot is the same: I find myself irresistibly moved to assent to the claim in question when it is proposed to me. I cannot deliberate and then decide whether to believe it or not. When I find myself assenting to some claim (believing it, taking it as true), then, my assent typically does not involve choice or deliberation. It is simply given to me.

But not all claims will produce acts of assent in this way when they are proposed. Some will provoke assent to their contradictories: when faced with the claim *genocide is a proper instrument of foreign policy* you probably find yourself involuntarily assenting to the claim *it is not the case that genocide is a proper instrument of foreign policy*, which is the contradictory of the first claim. Some claims will provoke other attitudes, such as puzzlement, incomprehension, or doubt. When faced with the claim *every even number can be expressed as the sum of two primes*, for instance, I find myself moved to assent neither to it nor to its contradictory. Rather, I am puzzled because the claim seems neither true nor false to me (which isn't to say that it is neither true nor false, only that I don't know which it is). In this case, while I assent neither to the claim nor to its contradictory, I do assent to a derivative of it, which is *possibly every even number can be expressed as the sum of two primes*. And it will usually (perhaps always) be possible to express lack of direct assent when faced with some claim in the form of direct assent to some related or derived claim. Consider *the present King of France is bald*. I assent neither to it nor to its contradictory (because there is no present King of France), but I do assent to the claim *"the present King of France is bald" is puzzling*. Or, consider *the colorless green grass sighs aggressively*. In this case I find myself assenting to *"the colorless green grass sighs aggressively" is incomprehensible*. And so on.

The important (and controversial) point about acts of assent for the purposes of this book is that they are involuntary. You cannot decide to make them for they are quite beyond your direct control. If you find yourself assenting to the claim *this is the Lamb of God* when the priest elevates the host after the words of consecration have been spoken, then you just do. This is a fact about you at that time, like your sex or your age or the color of your skin. It probably means that you're a Christian. Likewise, if you find yourself assenting to the claim *this person is inferior to me* when faced with a person whose skin color is different from your own, then you just do. This is a fact about you that probably means you're a racist.

None of this means that you are without responsibility for your acts of assent. They will very often be traceable to events and decisions in your past for which you do bear responsibility – perhaps the decision to associate with Christians, or with racists. But the involuntary nature of all assents does mean that, in the sphere of religion, it is not sensible to think that you can simply decide to assent (to believe, to take as true): you cannot. The religious assents you do make or do not make at a particular time are vitally important features of your religiosity at that time – of the form of religious life that in fact you inhabit. But they're not features of you susceptible of quick or easy change, much less of change by voluntary fiat. I can decide to get up from my chair; I cannot decide to assent to the claim that Muhammad is the prophet of God.

This point brings us to acts of acceptance. These are distinct from acts of assent, at least with respect to the fact that they are subject to voluntary control: you can decide to make them. If you accept a religious (or any) claim, you entertain it as you might entertain a guest. That is, you invite the claim into your cognitive house (the house of your beliefs), you treat it as someone you're glad to have there, you nourish it, order your actions in relation to it, and generally make it at home. And you do all this entirely without respect to how you feel about the guest. Some guests you like and respect, others you despise and are repelled by; and these responses are very largely involuntary. But no matter what your involuntary responses to a particular guest might be, you can still decide to treat her as a guest.

So also with accepting a claim. By definition, a claim that you accept will not be one that you assent to. If you did assent to it, you wouldn't need to accept it, just as you wouldn't need to decide to treat someone as a guest if you already (and involuntarily) felt the liking that spontaneously produces hospitality. So the set of claims that you accept at a particular time will not include any that you assent to. Acceptance requires choosing to treat a claim as true (if it's the kind of claim that can be so treated), or choosing to take a claim as a guide for your life (if it's that sort of claim). Such acts of choice do not require that the claim in question seem true to you, or that it seem a proper guide for your life; they require only that you treat the claim as if it had whichever of these properties is appropriate. It will often naturally follow, with time and the establishment of certain habits, that claims you've accepted become claims you assent to. We are creatures of habit, and if we establish the habit of treating a claim as if it were of central importance to us, it will typically not be long before it comes to seem so.

An example. Suppose that, when faced with the claim *the Buddha is the unsurpassed refuge for suffering humanity* you do not assent to it. Perhaps it seems to you empty of meaning, or not obviously true, or seems to be something that may be of importance to others but not to you. Suppose, too, that there are pressing external reasons that cause you to decide to accept this claim in spite of your lack of assent to it. Perhaps you've married someone for whom it is a claim of central importance, or perhaps all your friends assent to it and seem happy as a result of doing so. And so you do accept it. Such acceptance, you rapidly discover, involves other actions: chanting the triple refuge daily (I take refuge in the Buddha/I take refuge in his doctrine/I take refuge in his monastic community), giving gifts to monks and receiving teaching from them, and so on. It is not long before you find yourself not only accepting but also assenting to *the Buddha is the unsurpassed refuge for suffering humanity*. The action of acceptance will then have produced the response of assent. This is not an inevitable progression, but it is certainly a common one given the depth and rapidity with which habit affects cognitive life.

Accepting a claim will not, however, always lead to assent. Much will depend on other factors: the pressure of events, the presence of other, conflicting habits, the presence or absence of supportive others with like habits, and so on. Solitary attempts to establish assent-producing habits are much more likely to fail than those undertaken along with others doing the same. Nonetheless, there is a strong link between undertaking to accept a claim and coming, with time, to assent to it.

Neither assent nor acceptance is a single, univocal category. It is, for example, possible to assent to a claim with joy ("I'm very glad I believe that") as well as with deep regret ("I very much wish I didn't believe that"). Assents may also be differentiated according to the importance they have for those who make them, and according to the depth and complexity of the connections they have with other assents. For example, I assent to both *God is loving me now* and *Chicago is at roughly the same latitude as Rome* in the sense that when faced with either claim I find myself at once and involuntarily taking it as true. But the former is of central importance for me, and is deeply and complicatedly articulated and interwoven with other beliefs I have. The latter, by contrast, is relatively insignificant for me: I have little invested in it, and it remains at the periphery of the web of my beliefs. Not much would change for me, cognitively speaking, were I to cease to believe that Chicago is at the same latitude as Rome. A great deal would change were I to cease to believe that God is loving me now.

Assents may also be discriminated one from another by the extent to which they seem (to those who make them) to be non-negotiable or incapable of change. For some of the assents I make it is easy for me to imagine a scenario in which I would no longer make them. Faced with relevant and authoritative information I can imagine ceasing to assent to the claim that more people currently live in Mexico City than in Jakarta (although I currently believe this to be true). But I cannot easily imagine a scenario in which I would cease to assent to the claim that my wife is a human being (what evidence or argument should convince me that she is an android?), or to the claim *God is loving me now* (should my sufferings lead me to be more blasphemous than Job?). Assents are not, then, all alike in the non-negotiability they appear to have for those who make them; and those that appear profoundly non-negotiable are also likely to be those that seem cognitively important and deeply interwoven with other assents. Specifically religious assents, belonging as they do to an account of things that seems comprehensive, incapable of abandonment, and central to those who offer it, are likely to be high on the scale of non-negotiability, and high, too, on the scale of importance and depth of articulation with other beliefs.

Acceptances, too (entertaining claims without assenting to them) are not all alike. Some are tentative, engaged in with the thought that they might soon be abandoned. Of this sort are my experiments in supporting the Chicago White Sox: I entertain the claims that go with such support along with the accompanying thought that I might well soon cease to do so. But things are not the same with my entertainment of the claim *I am not a liar.* I don't assent to this claim (it doesn't seem true to me) because I know that too often I lie. But my entertainment of it is not tentative because I do assent (non-negotiably, even religiously) to the claim *I ought not to be a liar,* and entertaining the claim *I am not a liar* is one of the instruments that will (I think) help it increasingly to become true that I am not. This example suggests a broader truth, which is that acts of acceptance that have to do with a religious account of things are more likely to be non-tentative than otherwise, and than other kinds of acceptance.

What's just been said is scarcely an exhaustive account of the nature of assents and acceptances. It passes rather lightly over some difficult and interesting questions in epistemology proper, some of which I'll return to in chapter 3. The point of most importance at this stage is that assent and acceptance differ, and that inhabiting a religious form of life typically requires only the latter, even though it may also value the former. It will suffice, for instance, to inhabit Catholic Christianity, to accept the teachings of the Church; assent is an added grace and delight, not a requirement. Catholic Christians will likely add that even the decision to accept is the one for which God's special grace is needed.

To summarize the argument of this chapter so far: I've suggested that inhabitants of a religion cannot avoid accepting at least some religious claims as a condition of their habitation; that religions may differ greatly as to the importance they allot to such acceptance; that religions typically require acceptance of claims central to or definitive of them (I called such claims *doctrines*), and suggest acceptance of claims peripheral to them (I called such claims *teachings*); and that acceptance of a claim is voluntary, while assent to it is not. All this is by way of necessary preface to a consideration of the questions about truth raised by religious diversity.

## 2.3 Truth, Falsehood, Incompatibility

Truth, I shall take it in what follows, is something that claims may have. This may be put grammatically: the predicate *is true* and its complement *is false* (together with appropriate modifiers) have claims (doctrines, teachings) as their proper subjects. Consider the claim *there is one God*, which is indisputably a doctrine of many religions (most Christian, Jewish, and Islamic forms of life, at least). This claim can have the predicate *is true* attached to it, yielding *"there is one God" is true*, or (equivalently) *it is true that there is one God*. It can also have the predicates *is possibly true* or *is necessarily true* attached to it. The use of the former yields the claim that perhaps (maybe, it is not impossible that) there is one God; the use of the latter yields the claim that it must be the case (certainly, inevitably, incontrovertibly) that there is one God. Likewise, the doctrine in question may have the predicates *is false*, *is possibly false*, and *is necessarily false* attached to it.

It may be very difficult in the case of any particular doctrine to sort out what it means and which of these predicates should be applied to it. You may, for instance, find yourself in the condition of not assenting to or choosing any of the six claims yielded by applying the six predicates mentioned to the claim *there is one God*; perhaps you find yourself assenting to the claim *I have no idea what "there is one God" means*, or to the claim *"there is one God" isn't worth thinking about*. But you are not thereby compelled to assent to the claim *none of the six predicates ought ever be applied to "there is one God."* You might, after all, think that if you were to come to understand what *there is one God* means, you'd then be able to attach to it one or another of the predicates having to do with truth and falsehood. But some have argued that there are some locutions (some kinds of claim) to which none of these predicates either are or ought ever to be applied (possibly my earlier example, *the colorless green grass sighs aggressively*, is one such), and have further suggested that religious claims are often or always of this sort. But it is sufficiently obvious that, on the understanding of religion in play in this book, this is not the case – that inhabitants of religious forms of life do in fact make claims that rightly seem to them to be capable of having the predicate *is true* attached – that I shall not argue that case any further here.

Claims that belong to a religion (doctrines and teachings), therefore, typically may be true or false. Given the distinction already made between assent and acceptance, it doesn't follow that the inhabitants of any

particular religion will take all (or even any) of the doctrines of that religion to be true. This is so because *taking to be true* is characteristic of assent
but not of acceptance, and it is perfectly possible to inhabit a religion on
the basis only of acceptance. Nevertheless, it is typical that religions do
present their doctrines as true and assent to them as desirable; it is probably also the case that many religious people do assent to the doctrines
that belong to their religion; and it is certainly the case that no religious
person happily assents to a claim that seems to her to contradict any of
her religion's doctrines. To do this would (usually) be to cease to inhabit
the religion in question.

With all these qualifications in view it is now finally possible to address
the question about truth raised by religious diversity. This question is fundamentally a simple one: There are (or at the very least there appear to
be) conflicts or incompatibilities among the doctrines of different religions;
what is the proper response to this state of affairs? Notice that this is not,
in the first instance, a question about the truth of any particular religious
claim; questions of that sort may and do arise quite without reference to
religious diversity. It is, rather, a question about the proper response to the
bare fact of apparent conflict or incompatibility among the doctrines of
different religions. Before exploring answers to this question, it is important to say something about the kinds of incompatibility that may be found
among the doctrines of different religions. Among these I distinguish
three: contradictoriness, contrariety, and noncompossibility. Some brief
comments on each follow.

Two religious claims are contradictory if and only if each makes a claim
to truth, both cannot be true, and yet one must be true. You can most
easily find the contradictory of any claim by prefixing to it the phrase "it
is not the case that." So, the contradictory of the claim *there is no God but
God and Muhammad is the prophet of God* is *it is not the case that there is no
God but God and Muhammad is the prophet of God*. Similarly, the contradictory of *everyone ought to abide by the ten commandments* is *it is not the case
that everyone ought to abide by the ten commandments*. An equivalent of
this last claim is *there is at least one person who need not abide by the ten
commandments*.

Instances of exact contradictories among religious claims appear not to
be all that common. This is because in order for one religion to have *p*
among its doctrines (where *p* is any claim at all), and another to have *it
is not the case that p* among its, it will usually have to be the case that the
latter religion (or at least those of its adherents charged with formulating
doctrine) knows of the former and its doctrines, and is explicitly and self-

consciously concerned to reject *p*. It is of course possible that exact contradictories might be found among the doctrines of two religions in the
absence of this state of affairs; but it is less likely, and no examples spring
rapidly to mind.

Approximate contradictories are much more common. Two claims that
bear this relation one to another do not have the formal appearance of
contradictories, but can readily be made to yield a contradiction. For
example, Ratnakīrti, an eleventh-century Indian Buddhist philosopher,
composed a work whose central thesis is *whatever exists is momentary*.[4] A
strong case can be made (though I shall not make it) that this claim was
doctrinal for Ratnakīrti, and for the religious form of life inhabited by
many Indian Buddhist thinkers. The Christian scriptures affirm, in the
exhortations that come at the end of the Letter to the Hebrews, that Jesus
Christ is "the same yesterday, and today, and for ever" (13:8). It would not
be difficult to construct a short argument whose conclusion is that
Ratnakīrti's thesis entails the contradictory of Hebrews 13:8, and if this is
so, it also follows that Ratnakīrti's thesis and Hebrews 13:8 are approximate contradictories. And, of course, Ratnakīrti did not know the Letter
to the Hebrews, and whoever composed it did not know Ratnakīrti's
work, so neither thesis was constructed with the aim of contradicting the
other, even though this was the result.

There are, however, some exact (or virtually exact) contradictories to
be found among religious claims on the basis of just the kind of direct
historical connection mentioned. One famous example is the Qur'an's
claim that God is neither begotten nor begets.[5] This claim is probably to
be understood in part as a direct response to and rejection of the Christian claim that Jesus Christ was begotten by God, a claim that is both biblical (it is found in the first chapter of both Matthew's and Luke's Gospels)
and creedal (it is found in the Apostles' and Nicene Creeds). In this case,
then, Muslims propound the doctrine *God does not beget* and Christians
the doctrine *God begets Jesus*, which are not far from direct contradictories and are so because the former claim was framed in part precisely to
contradict the latter.

Contrariety, the second form of incompatibility among religious claims,
is more common than contradictoriness. Two religious claims are contrary
if and only if each makes a claim to truth, both cannot be true, and neither
need be. A simple example: If you claim that William Jefferson Clinton
ought to have been subjected to impeachment proceedings in 1998 and
I claim that no sitting United States President ought ever to be subjected
to impeachment proceedings, then we cannot both be right, for it is an

entailment of my claim that yours is false, and an entailment of yours that mine is false. But we can both be wrong: perhaps Clinton ought not to have been subjected to impeachment proceedings (in which case you're wrong), and yet some sitting presidents ought to be so subjected (in which case I'm wrong).

There are very many instances of what looks like contrariety among religious claims. Some Buddhists seem to propound with doctrinal force the claim *Gautama Śākyamuni is supreme among humans*; and some Christians appear to propound with doctrinal force the claim *Jesus of Nazareth is supreme among humans*. Some religious (but misguided) followers of the Chicago Cubs teach that the Cubs will win the World Series next year; more sensible people teach that the White Sox will win the World Series next year (though hardly anyone has ever seriously claimed that either the Sox or the Cubs will win the World Series this year). These and other like examples provide instances of contrary claims: both cannot be true, yet it is possible that neither is.

A third kind of incompatibility among religious claims is noncompossibility. Two claims are noncompossible if each prescribes a course of action and it is impossible for a single person to perform both. An everyday example: *live in England for more than half of each year* and *live in the United States for more than half of each year*. There are many religious claims that appear to bear this relation one to another. Consider *give all your surplus resources to the Church* and *give all your surplus resources to the Buddhist monastic community*; or *read the Bible as if it were the most important book in the world* and *read the Qur'an as if it were the most important book in the world*. It is impossible so to read both the Bible and the Qur'an, just as it is impossible to give all your surplus resources simultaneously both to the Church and to the Buddhist monastic order.

This kind of incompatibility indicates an important general truth about being religious. It is that no one can inhabit more than one form of religious life at a time. Religions bear the relation of noncompossibility one to another. This is because a form of life that seems to you comprehensive, incapable of abandonment, and of central importance to the ordering of your life (your religion, if you are fortunate enough to have one) by definition provides answers to (or at least a mode of addressing) those questions that seem to you of central importance to the ordering of your life. Such questions might include: Should I kill other humans? Is sensual pleasure the highest human good? Are there duties to God? – and so on. Simultaneous assent to or acceptance of different answers to these questions is both practically and logically impossible, from which it follows that simultaneous habitation of more than one religion is also impossible. Of course, serial habitation of different religions is possible; but being religious, while it lasts, is a monogamous affair.

There are other kinds of incompatibility that may obtain among religious claims, but these are the three most significant so far as the question of truth is concerned. It is the fact that there really are contradictory, contrary, and noncompossible religious claims that raises in especially sharp form the question of the truth of such claims in general. But here a note of warning needs to be sounded. The fact that some particular alien religious claim seems to be incompatible with some claim that belongs to the home religion (if you have one), or with some other alien religious claim (if you are not religious), does not mean that it actually is. It is enormously difficult to come to a good understanding of what an alien claim means, especially when, as is often the case, it is deeply embedded in a complex and highly ramified account of things. Consider the example of Ratnakīrti's claim *everything that exists is momentary*. This claim is part of a tradition of scholastic argumentation and system-building that was developed by more than a thousand years of intense intellectual work. A full understanding of what it meant in its eleventh-century Indian context is not easily had by someone to whom that context is alien, and it follows from this that any judgment made by such a person about this claim's incompatibility (or, indeed, its compatibility) with any other claim ought to be made with modesty and tentativeness. It's difficult enough to know what the doctrines and teachings of the home religion amount to; the difficulty of knowing what those of an alien religion come to is immense. The same difficulty would be encountered by a Buddhist attempting to understand what Christians mean by saying things like *God is three persons in one substance*.

It must also be emphasized that, in addition to the evidence for incompatibility among religious claims, there is also much evidence of compatibility. Some claims propounded with doctrinal force by Christians, for instance, seem at first blush identical with some so propounded by Jews. Consider *God created the world* as an example. Some claims propounded with doctrinal force by Buddhists, for example *one should make pilgrimage to places where the relics of Buddha are found*, are not identical with any religious claim made by Muslims, but are also not immediately or obviously either contrary to or noncompossible with such claims. Again, the extent and significance of compatibility among claims belonging to different religions is a matter for study; but its occurrence is beyond doubt.

This brief consideration of kinds of incompatibility returns us to the central question about the truth of religious claims raised by religious diversity. What, in the context of considering the truth of religious claims, is the proper response to the fact that there are incompatibilities among religious claims?

A common-sense response to this question is that not all religious claims are (or can be) true. This response treats incompatibilities among religious claims in the same way that most of us would treat incompatibilities among ordinary descriptive claims (Jane is taller than Mary/Mary is taller than Jane), or those about the best way to do something (in order to learn Latin it's essential to study grammar and syntax/in order to learn Latin it isn't essential to study grammar and syntax). Incompatibilities of this sort, it seems to most who have not been corrupted by philosophy, suggest difference with respect to truth: it isn't possible that both of the sentences about Jane and Mary are true, just as it isn't possible that both of the sentences about the best way to learn Latin are true. It may not always be obvious which of a pair of apparently incompatible sentences is true; but if the appearance of incompatibility turns out to be genuine, it will follow that both of them cannot be true. So runs the common-sense response, and a response of this sort is often made to the apparent incompatibilities among religious claims.

But there is also another kind of response to the question of truth. It refuses to make distinctions among religious claims with respect to their truth, saying instead that all religious claims are on a par in this respect – that they are all related identically to the predicate *is true* (and therefore also to the predicate *is false*). This response does not make the same immediate appeal to common sense as did that summarized in the preceding paragraph. How sensible can it be to say that *God begets* and *God does not beget* are related identically to the predicate *is true*? How sensible can it be, to put the same point differently, to say that *God begets* and *God does not beget* are both true (or both false)? In spite of this seeming difficulty, there are serious defenses of the view that all religious claims are on a par with respect to truth.

The two most influential views of this sort stem from the thought of the philosophers Immanuel Kant (1724–1804) and Ludwig Wittgenstein (1889–1951). The Kantian and Wittgensteinean ways of arriving at the view that all religious claims are on a par with respect to truth are deeply different; but they are similar in that each proceeds by defining what a religious claim is quite narrowly (much more narrowly than in this book), and by making sure that the criteria used to separate religious claims from others are capable of making it plausible that all the claims so separated are on a par with respect to truth.

## 2.4   Parity with Respect to Truth: A Kantian View

The simplest way in which it could be the case that all religious claims are on a par with respect to truth is that they all teach the same thing – that they all make the same claim. Suppose, to take a nonreligious analogy, that all economists were to teach only that rational-choice theory is true (the theory that everyone makes each of their economically-significant choices based solely upon rational calculation as to what will most benefit them). Then every member of the set of economic doctrines would be on a par with every other member because there would be no significant differences among them with respect to what they claim. There might, of course, be differences of other kinds: some economic doctrines might be expressed in French and some in Chinese; some in iambic pentameters and some in textbook prose. But differences of this sort would not affect the truth-value of the doctrines in question.

It is of course not the case that all economic doctrines make essentially the same claim. Economics, perhaps more than most disciplines, is riven with dispute and disagreement. But the same appears at first blush to be true of religions: their claims, as we've seen, appear sometimes to be incompatible. The burden of proof is then firmly upon those who want to say that all religious claims are substantively identical; and it does not seem to be an easy burden to bear.

Attempts to bear it almost always involve the construction and use of a principle of selection. Such a principle will permit its users to admit that not every religious doctrine claims the same thing, but still to say that there is some subset of the vast array of religious claims, some selection from its members, each and every member of which does teach the same thing or make the same claim. It will usually be added that the doctrines selected are the ones that really matter, the ones that are at the heart of, or constitute the essence of, all religions. It will then follow that all essential religious doctrines are on a par with respect to truth because they all do say the same thing.

Immanuel Kant's version of this strategy begins by making a distinction between "pure religious faith," which is "a plain rational faith which can be convincingly communicated to everyone," and "historical faith," which is intimately linked with particular historical forms (eighteenth-century Prussian pietistic Lutheranism in the case most familiar to Kant), and may be neither comprehensible nor convincing outside the particular location in which it is found.[6] The essential content of the former, of pure religious faith, is the understanding of all moral duties as given by God. This content – the claim *all moral duties are given by God* – is, according to Kant, present in all particular religions, all historical faiths, though not always with the same degree of explicitness and often overlaid by and connected with other doctrines and practices that do not cohere very well with it. Kant does not understand this claim as referring in any direct way to God; he understands the claim, rather, as an indication of the incapacity of human reason to arrive at any such direct descriptions. The claim is, in his preferred language, a necessary postulate of the practical reason – something we must think in order to make sense of what we know about moral duty. A full-dress explanation of Kant's thought on religion would require exposition of what it means to call something a necessary postulate of practical reason. But since I don't intend any such explanation here, it will suffice to focus on a single aspect of Kant's thought – that which discriminates between the fundamental religious claim, the "plain rational faith" which is always and everywhere the same, and the peripheral religious claims, which vary and may indeed be incompatible.

The fundamental religious claim is, according to Kant, discoverable and justifiable by reason alone, unaided by revelation, scripture, authoritative church teachings, or any other extraordinary means available only to a few. This means that the particulars of specific religions (the forms and beliefs of, say, Hinduism or Buddhism) cannot be essential to the discovery and justification of what is essential to religion, for this – the claim, recall, that all moral duties are given by God – is related to them only contingently. Religion, for Kant, is then "not a public condition; each human being can become conscious of the advances which he has made in this faith only for himself."[7] It has no history, and is always and everywhere the same – "one, immutable, and pure."[8]

Religious forms that do have a history (the institutions of the Catholic Church, say, or those of Orthodox Judaism) are on this view of value only so far as they aid individuals in coming to a proper understanding of and assent to the fundamental religious claim; this means also that the historical forms are valuable just to the extent that they do not substitute their own irredeemably particular claims and practices for the fundamental religious claim. The ideal Kantian religion, then, is one that exhibits an understanding of the insufficiency of its own particulars and recommends this understanding to its inhabitants.

This is a bare-bones version of the Kantian view of religion, and is scarcely adequate even as such. But it does serve to indicate one way in which the conclusion that all religious doctrines are on a par with respect to truth can be reached. This conclusion is reached by Kant by way of a radical separation of historically particular religious claims (which are on his view religious only by courtesy, as it were) from the single fundamentally and properly religious claim, which is that all moral duties are given by God. This claim, for Kant, is both true and that which all particular religious claims express more or less well. And it is in this limited sense that all religious doctrines are on a par with respect to truth. Even this claim – the claim that all moral duties are given by God – is not understood by Kant as a substantive claim about the nature of God. It is, rather, a purely formal claim intended to represent the impossibility of humans knowing anything about God's nature. But this point, although essential for a proper understanding of Kant's thought about religion in its own terms, doesn't affect the issue under discussion here.

Kant's principle of selection among religious claims is quite radical. Specifically Jewish claims about the ritual implications of the Torah are not, on this view, essentially or properly religious; neither are specifically Buddhist claims about the propriety of giving to the monastic order, or about the desirability of practicing certain forms of meditation. Kant thus characterizes very few of the claims likely to be thought of by religious people as centrally important to the practice of their religion as properly religious. He defines the endless variety of religious claims – claims about Muhammad, about Jesus, about Buddha, about the benefits and delights of prayer, of fasting, of eating, of celibacy, of sexual activity, and so endlessly on – down to a singularity, and argues that this single claim, the constitutive religious claim, is both true and essential to all actual religions. Variety and incompatibility among claims that seem religiously important to religious people is irrelevant to the truth of the single claim that really matters, religiously speaking.

This general strategy for answering the question of truth raised by religious diversity is not found only in the thought of Immanuel Kant. It also has contemporary advocates and defenders, and while these differ among themselves (and from Kant) on many particulars, they share the broadly Kantian tendency to divide claims that are proper or essential to religion from those that are not; to locate incompatibility among claims of the second kind; and to say that the claim (if, following Kant, there's only one), or claims (if there's more than one) of the first kind are on a par with respect to truth.

One influential contemporary advocate of a broadly Kantian strategy on this matter is John Hick, a British philosopher of religion who has written a great deal on the philosophical questions associated with religious diversity. On the question of truth and religious diversity, Hick acknowledges that there are indeed genuine differences and (at least apparent) incompatibilities among the claims of different religious communities, and he divides these differences into three categories.

The first category is disagreement about historical questions, questions that could (in principle if not in practice) be settled by appeal to historical fact. The examples Hick mentions include: Did Jesus of Nazareth die on the cross (Muslims think he did not; Christians think he did)? This is a historical question, thinks Hick, because it would in principle be possible to resolve it on the basis of sufficiently accurate information – a complete and detailed set of data on Jesus' vital signs from the moment of being nailed to the cross from the moment he was taken down from it. This data is of course not available; but if it were, it would resolve the question. Hick acknowledges, then, that there are genuine incompatibilities among religious claims of a historical sort, and that these cannot therefore all be on a par with respect to truth.

Hick's second category is disagreement about "quasi-historical or trans-historical,"[9] matters such as what happens when you die. Are you reincarnated, born again into another life on earth? Or do you enter heaven (or hell) immediately upon death? Or may you enter purgatory, an intermediate state between death and rebirth, or the world of the ancestors? Hick takes disagreements about these matters, too, to be genuine, to have to do with questions of fact. Apparent incompatibilities between claims on such matters may therefore be real: it can't be the case both that you'll immediately be reborn in another human life when you die, and that you won't immediately be so reborn. But disagreements about such matters, thinks Hick, are likely to be even more difficult of resolution than disagreements about the kinds of historical questions mentioned in the preceding paragraph. He says: "[T]he basic question of fact is so difficult to determine that it may well go on being discussed and disagreed about for a very long time or even for the rest of earthly history."[10] In the case mentioned, presumably, decisive evidence is available not historically, but only eschatologically, when all things are resolved at the end of time. This difficulty of resolution does not, however, remove the possibility that there might be genuine incompatibility among religious claims on such matters.

Hick's third category comprises differences in "ways of conceiving and experiencing, and hence also of responding to, the divine Reality."[11] Some religions claim that God is a person; others that what is of final and ultimate significance is non-personal, calling it Nirvana, or Emptiness, or Brahman-without-qualities. These are certainly different claims about what is religiously ultimate, and they appear at first blush also to be incompatible, as Hick acknowledges. But it is in his strategy for dealing with this kind of incompatibility that Hick's Kantian lineage becomes apparent. First, he makes a distinction between the ultimately religiously Real (he prefers the upper-case "R" to indicate the importance of this category) as it is in itself, on the one hand, and as it is experienced by us, on the other. Variation and apparent incompatibility are located at the second level; unity at the first. Second, he makes an equally Kantian epistemological move: we "are always aware of reality beyond ourselves in terms of the sets of concepts which structure our own cognitive consciousness."[12] This is an explanation for the variety in human understandings of and claims about what is ultimately real; it is a variety that ought to be expected (and is indeed unavoidable) because of the necessarily limited, historically located, and therefore contingent nature of each of our understandings, and of the tools we bring to the construction and defense of the claims we make.

The upshot of Hick's analysis of conflicting claims to religious truth is that there can be and is genuine incompatibility in what different religions claim about what has happened in the past, what will happen in the future, the nature of human persons, and the nature of the environment in which we find ourselves. But these incompatibilities are not religiously important. They do not make an important difference to what religion is really all about, which is "the transformation of human existence from self-centredness to Reality-centredness."[13] There is a precise formal analogy here with the Kantian location of what is really important about religion in the claim that all moral duties are given by God. It is not that Hick agrees with Kant in all respects about the nature of moral duty and its relation to theism; it is, rather, that he agrees with him about the use of a principle of selection that permits (and perhaps even requires) the conclusion that genuine incompatibilities among religious claims with respect to truth are not, in the end, of any real religious significance.

For those who follow the broadly Kantian strategy identified here, then, all genuinely religious claims are on a par with respect to truth. For Kant, this is because all contingent historical claims are not genuinely religious, even though they may be thought religiously significant by those who make them; and the rest may all be adequately expressed by the single claim *all moral duties are given by God*, which is just true (though in the complicatedly Kantian sense of being a necessary postulate of practical reason). For Hick, it is because religion (and therefore the making of religious claims) is really about the attainment of salvation or liberation (the final goal of all people, whether they know it or not), and differences about matters that have to do with historical or quasi-historical matters (Hick's first two categories, discussed above), while genuine, cannot and therefore do not affect what is proper to religion. Differences at the third level, about what the religiously ultimate is like, are also not differences with respect to truth; they are differences only at the level of how we humans experience what is religiously ultimate. So, for Hick, the apparent incompatibility between the claims *the Real is personal* and *the Real is nonpersonal* is best understood not as a difference between two claims with different truth-values, but rather as one between two equally efficacious methods of conceiving what can (finally and completely) not be adequately conceived. All genuinely religious claims at the third level, then, are on a par with respect to truth. As Hick puts it: "Such differences . . . are not of great *religious* [his emphasis], i.e. soteriological, importance. For different groups can hold incompatible sets of theories all of which constitute intellectual frameworks within which the process of salvation/liberation can proceed."[14]

This Kantian view often goes with what its adherents like to call a pluralism with respect to the question of religious truth. That is, placing all genuinely religious claims on a par with respect to truth, as these approaches do, is likely to go along with the judgment that we ought to think of the doctrines and teachings of all actual religious communities as being on a par with respect to truth, as well. This is not because they are all true, nor because they are all false. Kant, indeed, thinks that most historical claims taken by Christians to be of religious importance, and most ethical claims so taken by Jews (to take only two examples), are false. And Hick, as we have seen, does not think that both Christians and Muslims can be right in all that they teach. But both Hick and Kant (and others who follow this broad strategy) also think that the claims of actual religious communities (recall that these claims are no more than religious-by-courtesy for thinkers in this tradition) all stand in roughly the same relation to what is religiously important.

Just what this relation is cannot easily be said; but perhaps it is something like the relation that descriptions of different faces of a multi-colored cube bear to the cube. Each description of a face will comprise both true and false statements: true ones to the extent that what it claims about the face it describes is true (claiming the cube is red when the face being described actually is red), and false ones to the extent that what is claimed about the cube as a whole is false of the cube as a whole (claiming the cube is red when only one of its faces is, the rest being other colors). Further, each description will (or at least may) contain true and false statements in approximately the same proportions. In something like this sense – the sense of a working hypothesis that may turn out to be correct – Kantian theorists about religious truth may be able to think of the claims of actual religious communities as on a par with respect to truth.

The merits of the two essential parts of the Kantian strategy here discussed – the reduction of all religious claims to a single fundamental claim; and the view that the claims of all actual religious communities bear approximately the same relation to this fundamental claim – must now briefly be considered.

The first part of the strategy is not compatible with the understanding of religion in play in this book. According to this understanding, genuinely religious claims cannot be separated from quasi-religious ones in a Kantian fashion. This is because religion is understood in this book in phenomenal terms, which is to say in terms of how forms of life of a certain sort seem to those who inhabit them. A Kantian dismissal of the doctrines and teaching of particular religions as in some sense not properly religious is therefore impossible: such a dismissal would amount to telling religious people that they misunderstand their religion. It may of course be the case that Kant is right that what he understands as the fundamental religious claim is true and all those that contradict it are false. But the motives and intentions governing his stipulative understanding of religion as having essentially only to do with this fundamental claim are not those governing the work to be done in this book. So the quick and easy Kantian response to the question of religious truth in the light of religious diversity, which is that there is finally only one religious claim and it is true, will not be followed here.

The second part of the strategy, the pluralistic position that the claims of all actual religious communities bear approximately the same relation to the fundamental religious claim (recall the descriptions of sides of a cube), is a little more complex. For both Kant and Hick, this position does permit the possibility that particular religious claims can be true, and that particular religious claims can be false. And this part of the position will be followed here; it is, as already noted, part of the ordinary common-sense response to the fact of incompatibility among religious claims. But there is also the view, clearly evident in Hick's thought, that, in aggregate, the claims made by every actual religious community (the claims of Christians, of Buddhists, of Jews, of Muslims, and so forth) bear the same amount of truth – or at least that this ought to be a working assumption.

This view will not be adopted here. If it is an empirical claim about what is in fact true of the aggregate of the claims made by every religious community, then decisions about its truth must await investigation. And while no one (certainly not the author of this book) has sufficient knowledge of the particulars of every religion to make well-grounded claims about this matter, what I know about the claims of actual religions (as understood in this book) strongly suggests that truth and falsehood are not equally distributed among them. There are religious communities, for instance, whose teachings appear to be organized around false claims about the nature and destiny of human beings, claims that may command or require mass murder or suicide. Consider the approximately 900 murders and suicides at Jonestown in Guyana in 1978, the plans for systematic violence at Rajneeshpuram in Oregon in the 1980s, the use of nerve gas in the Tokyo subway by Aum Shinrikyo in 1995, or the suicides of the Heaven's Gate community in California in 1997. The groups that planned these horrific events are certainly religious as these are understood in this book. But it seems hardly plausible to think that the distribution of truth and falsehood across the aggregate of their claims is the same as that in Orthodox Judaism, for example. Hick would probably agree with this, and would say that he is interested not in all religious communities, but only in the great "post-axial" religions (Buddhism, Hinduism, Jainism, Judaism, Christianity, Islam). It is to these, he says, that the working hypothesis of parity with respect to truth ought to be applied. But then the pluralistic hypothesis is no longer quite as pluralistic as it seems, for now some actual religions are excluded from the claim that the aggregate claims of all actual religions are related identically to the fundamental religious claim.

There is, then, no compelling reason to adopt either element of the broadly Kantian strategy for dealing with the question of religious truth in the light of religious diversity. Further, in terms of the understanding of religion in play here, there are many reasons not to.

## 2.5 Parity with Respect to Truth: A Wittgensteinean View

Another way of arriving at the conclusion that all religious claims are on
a par with respect to truth can be derived from Ludwig Wittgenstein's
understanding of the nature of religious belief.

In his lectures on that topic given at Cambridge in 1938 (or there-
abouts; the exact date is uncertain) Wittgenstein says this:

> Suppose someone were a believer and said: "I believe in a Last Judgement,"
> and I said: "Well, I'm not so sure. Possibly." You would say that there is an
> enormous gulf between us. If he said "There is a German aeroplane over-
> head," and I said "Possibly[.] I'm not so sure," you'd say we were fairly near.[15]

What does he mean? Well, he means at least that there are different ways
of contradicting people, and that seeing this can help in coming to a good
understanding of what religious claims are. If I say, "There's a German
aeroplane," and you say, "Maybe," it's natural to think that we're both treating the German-aeroplane claim in the same way, perhaps as a hypothesis that may or may not be true. It may be that I have better eyesight
than you, or know more about the shapes of aeroplanes; but we agree on
what would count as good evidence for the truth of the German-aeroplane claim, and on the sort of access we should have to that evidence in
order to be warranted in making the claim. This is why, as Wittgenstein
says, we are "fairly near" on the matter, even though I assent to $p$ and you
assent to *maybe p*.

But in the case of the (religious) claim *there will be a last judgment*, affir-
mations of precisely the same form, suggests Wittgenstein, may signal a
disagreement of quite a different kind. If I assent to the claim *there will be
a last judgment*, I am in Wittgenstein's view not treating it as a hypothesis
for which there happens to be sufficient evidence, or for the truth of
which there happen to be sufficiently good arguments. I am treating it as
an element (perhaps a key element) in a picture of the world that is non-
negotiable for me, framing all my assents and activities without being
subject to change or abandonment by appeal to evidence or argument. It
is just these features that make the picture a religious one (for Wittgenstein; but his understanding here is entirely compatible with that offered
in chapter 1) and the belief in question one whose object is a religious
claim. If, then, someone says, "Well, I'm not so sure," when faced with a
claim that someone else treats religiously, the two are separated in quite a
different way than are those who disagree, using that form of words, about

a claim both treat as a hypothesis. They are separated by an "enormous gulf" just because they differ about what ought to count in arriving at decisions to assent to the claim in question. If, then, you treat as a hypothesis a claim that I treat religiously, we think very differently about the claim. We have, as Wittgenstein might put it, different pictures; or we inhabit different forms of life.

The position just sketched might be generalized and extended in the following way (I leave open the question of whether Witttgenstein should be interpreted as so generalizing and extending it; the interpretation of his thought is a notoriously difficult matter). Suppose it is definitive of religious claims that evidence and argument are irrelevant to the function they have in the lives of those who assent to them. This would mean that appeal to evidence and argument have no bearing upon how it is that people who assent to them come to do so and continue to do so. If I treat *Jesus is the Christ* or *Buddha is the supreme refuge* as religious claims, and you suggest evidence that calls these claims into question, or arguments that (you think) make continued assent to them implausible, I will not be moved in my assent. Evidence and argument will be about as relevant to my religious assent as will appeals to what the Qur'an says for those without interest in or knowledge of that book.

Suppose, further, that being capable of support (or rebuttal) by evidence or argument is a necessary ingredient for being true. This would be to say that no claim can be true unless it is capable of support or rebuttal in these ways. It would then follow that no religious claim can be true. To put this rather differently: If it is only hypotheses that are capable of bearing the predicate *is true*, and if no religious claim is a hypothesis, then no religious claim is capable of bearing the predicate *is true*. And this is precisely the conclusion that no religious claim either is or can be true, which is also the view that all religious claims are on a par with respect to truth.

It is possible to put the argument of the preceding paragraph differently, and by so doing to make it accord more closely with Wittgenstein's thought. You might say that some forms of life use the predicate *is true* in connection only with hypotheses (in the sense of "hypothesis" just mentioned); and in those forms of life (perhaps they are scientific forms of life, or empiricist forms of life, or some such) religious claims cannot be true. But other forms of life (religious ones, let's suppose) use the predicate *is true* quite differently. In them, this predicate is applied only to claims taken by those who assent to them as absolute, non-negotiable, and insulated from evidence or argument – in other words, to Wittgensteinean religious beliefs. In these forms of life, then, only religious claims can possibly be bearers of the predicate *is true*. Hypotheses and other artifacts of science cannot. This way of putting the argument yields the conclusion *every religious claim must be true*, a conclusion that asserts nothing substantively different from *no religious claim can be true* (paradoxical though this seems) because a different understanding of what it is to use the predicate *is true* is in play in each statement.

Understanding religious claims as necessarily being true (on one understanding of what *is true* means), or as necessarily being false (on another), has most plausibility when taken as a proposition about the way in which some religious claims are assented to – a proposition, that is, about the peculiar way in which some claims are taken as true, rather than about the state of affairs that the claim seems to describe (if it's a descriptive claim), or to recommend (if it's a commendatory one). For there is no doubt that some claims are assented to in very much the way that Wittgenstein takes religious claims to be assented to. I, for example, assent to the claims *God loves me* and *my wife exists* in very much this way. That is, I have not arrived at my assent to these claims on the basis of evidence (at least, not on the basis of the kind of evidence that would be relevant to coming to assent to certain hypotheses in, say, inorganic chemistry); and they are, for me, entirely insulated from argument, which is roughly to say that I would reject any argument whose conclusion was that either of these claims is false solely on the ground that it had such a conclusion. I would do this, moreover, even if I could see nothing wrong with the argument.

It is also clearly the case that many religious claims (as these are understood in this book) are assented to in something very like this way, and that to see this is to see something of deep importance about religion, something pointed to in chapter 1 with the depiction of religious forms of life as seeming to their inhabitants to be incapable of abandonment. Religious people are not religious in the same way that most golfers play golf (as a matter of choice, recreation, and preference), nor in the way that most supporters of an increase in the minimum wage support this course of action (because it seems, more or less tentatively, to offer more promise than rival courses of action). Rather, they will often be willing both to die rather than abandon their religion and to kill in its defense.

But a broadly Wittgensteinean understanding of religious claims is not without its difficulties. Such an understanding focuses attention on the way in which a claim is assented to, on the adverbial aspect of religious assents, we might say. It explains very well what it means to assent to a claim religiously. But Wittgenstein may also mean that there is nothing more to say about the truth of claims assented to in this way, that there is no state of affairs that makes such assents true. And if he is so read, then it must be said that this is not how most religious believers understand their acts of assent. Religious believers may (and most do) think that the truth of the claims they assent to or accept is not to be understood exhaustively in terms of the peculiar mode in which they assent to or accept them; they typically think also that the claims to which they assent (claims about God, the Last Judgment, or the possibility of Nirvana) are true of the world.

This empirical point is important. Most religious communities appear to treat their doctrines and teachings not only as claims to be assented to in a non-hypothetical, non-negotiable fashion, but also as claims that are true in the sense that they accurately (or at least more accurately than not) describe the way things are, or commend what ought to be commended. This is evident in the fact that religious communities often do respond with argument when one of their doctrines is challenged. When, for instance, the Buddhist doctrine *everything that exists is momentary* was challenged as being untrue because incoherent by Hindu philosophers in India, Buddhists did not respond as a Wittgensteinean believer would: they did not, that is, point to the profound difference in the forms of life inhabited by Buddhists and Hindus, and shake their heads regretfully at the impossibility of communicating or coming to understand in what the difference consists. No, they argued: they defended both the coherence and the truth of their doctrine, and did so with arguments that they apparently expected to be comprehensible (and perhaps even convincing) to their interlocutors. And this kind of response, which has traditionally gone under the name of apologetics in the Christian world, appears to be typical of religious communities. A Wittgensteinean view of the necessary parity of religious claims with respect to truth does not, therefore, seem convincing as a description of how in fact religious claims are treated by those who assent to them.

Wittgenstein is himself partly aware of this empirical difficulty. He is aware, that is to say, that people who think of themselves as religious do sometimes treat the claims they take to be essential to their religion as susceptible of support by evidence and argument. In the *Lectures*, a certain Father O'Hara is mentioned as doing this. In so doing, says Wittgenstein, O'Hara makes religious belief a question of science, and this is to make the ludicrous error of trying to turn religious beliefs into something reasonable.[16] The strength of the language Wittgenstein uses in repudiating this view shows how fundamental an error it seems to him to be. It shows, also, that he is forced by his own views to adopt the position of telling religious people what they ought to think about their religiosity.

It's allowable, I think, that there are (or at least that there could be) forms of life in which the predicate *is true* is used in something like the broadly Wittgensteinean sense discussed. Such forms of life would understand *is true* to mean just and only *is asserted non-negotiably*, *is immune to evidence and argument*, and *is expressive of a basic orientation to life*. Perhaps the form of life inhabited by a paranoid schizophrenic whose fundamental delusion has to do with the idea that all medical doctors are agents of global Communism requires the use of the predicate *is true* in something like this sense. When a paranoid schizophrenic of this sort assents to (takes as true) the claim *this doctor is an agent of global Communism*, she is perhaps showing her intention to take the claim in all the ways just mentioned. She is, perhaps, primarily expressing some facts about her own cognitive structure and attitudes – that this claim expresses her basic life-orientation and is not further negotiable for her.

It's allowable, too, that there could be many forms of life of this sort, and that some of them could generate claims that appear at first glance to be incompatible with one another by being contradictory, contrary, or noncompossible. A form of life marked by obsessive-compulsive fixation upon the (supposed) fact that all doctors are in fact clandestine agents of the Microsoft Corporation will certainly generate claims that appear incompatible with those generated by the form of life mentioned in the preceding paragraph: doctors presumably can't all be both clandestine agents of global Communism and clandestine agents of the Microsoft Corporation. But given the way that truth is understood in these two forms of life, the conflict is no more than apparent; the apparently opposed claims turn out not to be about doctors at all, but rather to be expressive of facts about the cognitive lives of those who assert them. And insofar as they are to be so understood, they do possess parity with respect to truth.

If religious claims were, as some followers of Wittgenstein might claim, all of this sort, then the response to the central question of this chapter – Given the fact of religious diversity, what can reasonably be said about the truth of religious claims? – would be quick and easy. It would be that religious diversity raises no special problems with respect to the truth of religious claims, and that this is so because they are all necessarily on a par in this respect. Unfortunately, on the understanding of religion in play in this book (and on the self-understanding of most Christians, Buddhists,

Muslims, Jews, and so on) religious claims are not of this sort, and so this quick and easy response will not do.


## 2.6  Parity with Respect to Truth: Nonreligious Views

People who understand themselves as religious are much less likely than people who do not to answer the question of truth raised by religious diversity by saying that all religious claims are on a par with respect to truth. In this religious people are just like people with strong political convictions: it's hard to be a card-carrying Libertarian and to think that what Democrats claim about the proper ordering of the body politic is just as true as what Libertarians claim. So also, with appropriate changes, for practicing Jews or Muslims.

People who do think of themselves as religious and who yet want to adopt some kind of parity-response to the question of truth have to do some difficult work that always ends in making precisely the kinds of discrimination among religious claims with respect to truth that the work was designed to avoid. That is, they typically have to judge some apparently religious claims as not really religious (Kant would say this about a claim like *I must attend Mass weekly*), and in so judging to permit them to bear a different relation to truth than those they judge genuinely religious. Or, they must judge that while not all apparently religious claims are on a par with respect to truth, the most important ones (the ones that really count) are; and in so judging they repudiate the parity-response they are trying to defend.

But nonreligious people, those for whom all religions are alien, are more likely to find parity-responses attractive. In large part this is because it is quick and easy to place on a par the claims and practices of communities in which you have no personal interest and with none of which you identify. Those without musical interests are likely to place on a par the passions, concerns, and claims of devotees of chamber music and those of afficionados of country music. But a parity-response is also attractive because a posture of neutrality, of disinterested even-handedness with respect to particular religious claims, may seem to require just such a response. An agent of the United States charged with interpreting the religion clauses of the First Amendment may think it essential to proceed as if all religious claims are equally true. Docs not the First Amendment itself seem to require this? If it does, then someone charged with making law, or with specifying the constitutionality of law that has been made, will strive to act (at least in her legislative or judicial dress) as if all religious claims are indeed on a par with respect to truth. For doing otherwise will seem to offend against the letter of the law that governs the religion-neutral state.

On the understanding of religion in play in this book, however, it is impossible for the state consistently to legislate and to interpret the meaning of legislation as though all religious claims were on a par with respect to truth. A few examples will show this. The United States Supreme Court ruled in 1988 that a lower court's judgment that Native Americans may not use peyote in their religious rituals did not infringe their First Amendment rights to the free exercise of their religion, and was therefore constitutional and could stand. It made a similar ruling in 1968 about the propriety of using the force of law to require Jehovah's Witness parents, against their will and contrary to their religious beliefs, to permit doctors to give blood transfusions to their sick children. And in a string of rulings from 1895 onwards, it upheld the constitutionality of laws disenfranchising Latter-Day Saint (Mormon) polygamists and confiscating their property.[17]

It might be argued that the state acts in these cases not with any position on the truth of the claims mentioned but rather in response to what it takes to be its own overriding interests – in, for example, the preservation of the life of a child in the Jehovah's Witness cases). But even if this is the best way to understand the state's judgments and actions in such cases, it's easily possible to derive the fact that the state's action implies the falsehood of claims held to be true by some religious groups, even if such implication isn't in the forefront of the state's agents' intentions, nor ever made explicit by them. In all the cases I've mentioned, agents of the state acted as though some religious claims are, in the eyes of the state, false. In the peyote case, the claim in question may reasonably be thought to have been: *properly conducted religious ritual requires the use of peyote*. In the Jehovah's Witness case it might have been *God bans blood transfusions for some Americans*. And in the Latter-Day Saint cases it might have been: *God requires polygamy of some Americans*.

Could the state have acted as though, in its eyes, all these claims (and their contradictories) are on a par with respect to truth? It certainly could (and perhaps should) have interpreted the Constitution to permit peyote use to Native Americans, the refusal of transfused blood to Jehovah's Witnesses, and polygamy to Latter-Day Saints. But it could not consistently act as if both the following claims are true: *blood transfusion is always and everywhere impermissible* (which it may be that some Jehovah's

Witnesses believe), and *blood transfusion ought to be done whenever it can save a life* (which many Christians believe). The best the state that aspires to religious neutrality can do is to permit Jehovah's Witnesses to act in accord with their beliefs and Christians to act in accord with theirs (though the United States fails often even to do this). But so to permit is not to act as if the two beliefs just mentioned were on a par with respect to truth; it could not be, because the beliefs are at least contrary to one another, and with only a little work can be made to yield a direct contradiction.

This difficulty can most clearly be seen in the case of religious claims of universal scope that explicitly reject the possibility of religion-neutral legislation. Consider the following claim, one that might well be made by some Muslims: *All legislation ought explicitly to be written as implementation of what is commended by the Qur'an and the Hadith* (the Hadith are authoritative narrative reports of actions and sayings of Muhammad and his companions, originally handed down orally). This is a claim with respect to which legislative neutrality is impossible; such neutrality is, moreover, neither attempted nor achieved in the United States or in other states whose constitutions are in part based upon that of the United States. And such a claim is not hopelessly exotic or odd. Many actual religions make claims of just this sort.

Consistently acting from a nonreligious standpoint as though all religious claims are on a par with respect to truth is, then, no more possible than consistently so acting from a particular religious standpoint. This is so even though many modern states enshrine as constitutional the belief that so acting is both possible and desirable. As with the broadly Kantian response already discussed, the only way in which it can be made to seem possible consistently to act in this way is by selecting some small subset of actual religious claims, calling those genuinely and properly religious, and making sure that no member of this subset contradicts (or stands contrary to, or is noncompossible with) any other such member. Suppose, for instance, that the state's view of what constitutes a properly religious claim is governed by the following rule: *A claim is properly religious if and only if it is said to be so by those who assent to or accept it, and it conflicts with no law or interest of the state.* On this rule of recognition, it is possible consistently to act on the axiom that all religious claims are on a par with respect to truth, but the cost is that many claims thought to be of religious significance by religious people are by this rule judged to be not really religious. And although the rules deployed by self-described religion-neutral states for the recognition of religious claims are usually a little more nuanced than the one just given, they are of the same general kind, and they face the intractable problems faced by all such rules.

Views that place religious claims on a par with respect to truth from a nonreligious standpoint are, then, no more likely to succeed than those that do so from a religious one. This is so even though they are widespread and often written into law; neutrality with respect to religious truth is one of the chief burdens of the democracies of late modernity, and it is increasingly obvious that it cannot be borne.

The views about religious truth in the context of religious diversity so far canvassed have all attempted to place religious claims on a par with respect to truth. This is not the only kind of response; neither is it the most common. Far more common are responses that see some religious claims as true and others as false, responses that assert difference with respect to truth. These are, at least at first blush, common-sense responses; most people, when faced with a pair of contradictory claims, are likely to say that one must be false and the other true, even if they can't immediately tell which is which. This sort of response is especially attractive to religious people because they are likely to think that the doctrines of their religion are true, and by so thinking be inclined to claim that apparently contradictory teachings must be false. But there are varieties of response possible under this generic heading, and to these I now turn.

## 2.7 Difference with Respect to Religious Truth: Exclusivism

In the context of religious diversity, exclusivism is a response to the question of religious truth typically offered by the religiously committed – by those who have a home religion. Recall that the question of truth raised by learning about religious diversity is not the same as the question of salvation: the former has to do with whether the religious alien may be thought of as teaching anything true, and the latter with who gets saved and how. In this section I'll be dealing only with exclusivism as a response to the question of truth. On this question, then, exclusivists are concerned to emphasize that true religious claims are found only among the doctrines and teachings of the home religion, which is the same as to say that no alien religion has any true claims among its doctrines and teachings. This is the central exclusivist idea. It amounts to the view that, for whatever reason, the home religion is uniquely privileged with regard to the possession of religious truth. This highly desirable commodity is found, for exclusivists, only within the bounds of the home community: the market in it has been cornered, and so if you're an exclusivist and you want to know what is religiously true, you have only one place to look.

This view is not widely held. There are, I think, no instances of its being propounded as doctrine or teaching by any Christian, Jewish, Muslim, Hindu, Buddhist, Confucian, or Taoist community. The reason is not far to seek. The view commits anyone who holds it to the claim that no alien religious teaching is identical with any teaching of the home community. For if there were any such instance of identity, it would immediately follow that if the relevant teaching of the home religion is true, that of the alien religion must also be. Suppose the home religion teaches (truly, from the viewpoint of its members) that there is one God who is the only worship-worthy one. An exclusivist who belongs to such a community must then say that no alien religion teaches just this. A similar move would have to be made by exclusivists with respect to claims like *unrestricted violence is unacceptable*, and *sensual indulgence is not the highest human good*, claims which many religions will share.

While it is certainly a logical possibility that no religion other than the home religion makes any claim that the home religion makes, the reason why there are (for example) no Buddhist exclusivists in the sense under discussion is that Buddhists typically know very well that some of the claims they make are also made by religious aliens. Most Hindus and Jains, for example, agree with Buddhists that humans have more than one life – and Buddhists have often known this to be the case. Most Christians and Jews, moreover, teach that murder is unacceptable, as also do Buddhists. It is therefore difficult for a thoughtful Buddhist to be an exclusivist with respect to truth. It is at least equally difficult for Christians or Jews so to be, because of the fact (known to most Christians and most Jews) that so many of their teachings are held in common.

The difficulties for would-be exclusivists belonging to actual religious communities are made more acute by the fact that few such communities find any pressing need to teach exclusivism, or to require it of their members. Certainly it is possible to imagine a religion whose teachings are propounded not only as true but also as without remainder unique, neither taught nor agreed to by anyone else. But there seems to be no actual religion like this. Certainly, many (perhaps most) religions like to think of some of their teachings as true and unshared by others. Perhaps Christians think of trinitarian doctrine like this, or Buddhists think this regarding teachings about the significance of the monastic community. But none seem to want to think of all their teachings as being of this sort.

Hence, developed statements and defenses of an exclusivist response to the question of truth are not to be found.

It is worth noting, though, what a religion that did coherently and plausibly teach exclusivism with respect to truth would probably be like.

First, a religion with very few teachings and doctrines might plausibly be exclusivist. The greater in number a religion's teachings become, the more likely it is that some other religion also teaches one or more of them. If your religion teaches only that if you sneeze before you put your shoes on in the morning you must go back to bed, it is not unlikely that this teaching is unique, that no other religion duplicates it. Inhabitants of such a religion might plausibly teach exclusivism with respect to truth.

Second, a religion whose inhabitants are effectively isolated from knowledge that there are any alien religions might also plausibly teach exclusivism with respect to truth. This is so even if the religion's teachings are many, for in order for exclusivism with respect to truth to be or become implausible to the inhabitants of a religion, it will not suffice that there be alien religions whose teachings duplicate some of the home religion's teachings. It must also be the case that this is known or suspected. And for the inhabitants of an isolated religious form of life, such knowledge or suspicion might conceivably be lacking.

Few actual religions now meet the criteria mentioned in either of the preceding paragraphs, which is in part why few or none teach exclusivism with respect to truth. But there are also many other reasons why particular religions find the exclusivist response to the question of truth unacceptable, reasons internal to the religions in question. Jews, for instance, usually expect the God who made a covenant with Noah after the flood (Genesis 9) to have some kind of relationship with all humanity, and therefore usually expect that this relationship will find expression in the teaching of at least some truths about God by alien (in this case, non-Jewish) religions. Christians tend to believe that God has revealed something of himself to all people (the first two chapters of Paul's Letter to the Romans strongly suggest such a view), and are therefore typically puzzled by the suggestion that no alien (in this case non-Christian) religion teaches anything true about God.

The fact that there are religion-specific reasons for expecting exclusivism to be false (and many more of them than the two mentioned in the preceding paragraph) indicates a final distinction that must be made about exclusivism. It is the distinction between exclusivism as a necessity and exclusivism as an actual possibility. Those who assert exclusivism as a necessity (if there are any) say not only that exclusivism is true (that it occurs) but also that it must be true, that it would be incoherent to deny it. Those who assert exclusivism as an actual possibility say only that exclusivism is true (that it happens to obtain); they acknowledge that it would not be incoherent to deny it. Philosophers will say that this difference – the difference between those who say that exclusivism is and must be true, and those who say that it is but need not be true – is a modal difference. That is, it is a difference in the mode under which exclusivism is asserted: exclusivism may be asserted as a necessity (modalized as necessary); or it may be asserted as a possibility (modalized as possible). This is an important difference, for the claim *exclusivism is necessarily true* rules out *exclusivism could have been false*, while *exclusivism is possibly true* entails the possibility of (is indeed just another way of saying) *exclusivism could have been false*.

Since there are no serious defenders of either view it isn't necessary to spend more time on them here. But the difference between assertions under the mode of necessity and assertions under the mode of possibility should be noted here since it will recur later in the book.

While exclusivism is not a serious response to the question of religious truth raised by religious diversity, one of the impulses behind it requires some further comment. This is the impulse to declare the home religion especially privileged with respect to truth. Most religions share this impulse; it is evident, as we shall see, in inclusivist responses to the question of truth as well, and it flows quite naturally from what religious forms of life are like, which is, recall, to seem to those who belong to them to provide a complete, and centrally important account of things that cannot be abandoned. If you belong to a form of life of this sort, it is likely to seem to you that its teachings are both true and true in a quite special way, true in a way that no other set of claims is or could be. This natural and widespread part of being religious can be elucidated and systematized in a number of ways; exclusivism is only the most implausible and least widespread among these.

## 2.8 Difference with Respect to Religious Truth: Inclusivism

Inclusivists share with exclusivists the view that some religious claims are true and some false. They also share the view that the doctrines and teachings of the home religion are true and alien claims incompatible with them false. But inclusivists differ from at least necessitarian exclusivists on the question of whether there may be any true alien claims – the question of whether it is possible for an alien religion to include any true claim among its doctrines and teachings. Inclusivists take this to be a real possibility, as also do possibilist exclusivists; for necessitarian exclusivists, as we've seen, it is not thought to be possible. Inclusivists add to the view that alien claims may be true the position that the home religion teaches more religious truths, or teaches them more fully, than does any alien religion. These views together yield the characteristic inclusivist response to the question of truth, which is that the home religion is at the top of a hierarchy of truth-teaching religions; it includes their truths, if they teach any, in its truths, which is what provides the position's name.

Inclusivism on truth is a widely-held position: many actual religious communities include it among their teachings, and it is easy to see why. It honors one of the important intuitions of exclusivism, which is that the doctrines and teachings of the home religion must be especially privileged with respect to truth, by its claim that the home religion teaches more truth, or teaches it more fully, than does any alien religion. But it does this without committing itself to the deeply implausible necessitarian exclusivist view that no alien religion could (and therefore no alien religion does) teach anything true. Some version of inclusivism, then, is taught by most types of Buddhism, Hinduism, Islam, Judaism, and Christianity – and, no doubt by other religions as well. It is, for instance, the official teaching of the Roman Catholic Church.

The generic inclusivist position may be subdivided in a number of ways. First, the claim as to the presence of truths taught by alien religions may be made in the mode of necessity or of possibility, as we have also seen to be the case with exclusivism. And second, the relation between the truths taught within the home religion and those taught outside it may be specified differently: as closed if all alien truths are already taught by the home religion; and as open if it is possible that some are not.

The difference between asserting the characteristic claims of inclusivism as necessarily true and as possibly true is relatively straightforward. Suppose it is said necessarily to be the case that, first, some alien religious claims are true; and, second, that any particular set of alien religious truths is inferior or subsidiary to the truths taught by the home religion. Saying this – teaching inclusivism under the mode of necessity – will ordinarily (and perhaps always) be done because there is some other feature of the home religion's doctrines or teachings that requires it. Assessment of any particular example of it will therefore have to rest upon assessment of this other feature, whatever it turns out to be.

Consider the following Buddhist example (not so far as I can tell explicitly stated in Buddhist texts, but entirely compatible with what is said in some of the classical texts of Indian Buddhism). From the claims *only Buddha is omniscient* and *only Buddha is omnibenevolent* it is relatively easy to derive *Buddha teaches all the truths from which suffering humans can benefit*. A feature of omnibenevolence may be the desire to teach all the truths from which any sufferer can benefit; and a feature of omniscience may be knowing just which truths to teach to whom at what time. But suppose we now add the claim that Buddha does not withhold true teaching from non-Buddhists because his compassion does not permit such withholding. This might be understood as a necessary feature of Buddha, not one that he could possibly have been without. We might add the yet further claim that the best (only possible) way for Buddha to make true teachings available to non-Buddhists is by establishing (anonymously, of course) alien religious communities, communities of Hindus, Jains, and Confucians, for example. This might be so because only in communities whose members offer (as a result of being taught) accounts of things that seem to them comprehensive, unsurpassable, and of central importance (which is, recall, the definition of religion in play in this book) can true teachings that will remedy suffering be effectively made available. Finally, we might add the claim that those who have explicit knowledge of the teachings of Buddhism are, by definition, those who know more of what is true, religiously speaking, than those who do not. It will then easily follow that it is necessarily the case that at least some (and possibly all) non-Buddhist religions teach some truths; and that the truths they teach stand in a relation of incompleteness to the fuller set of truths taught by Buddha. No doubt many of the details of this sketchy argument cry out for elucidation; but its outlines should be clear, and it is of the generic kind offered by a good number of actual religions. Its upshot is that there are necessarily some true alien claims, and that this fact can be known independently of knowing the particulars of any alien claims.

Inclusivism may also, however, be taught without affirming that there must be some true alien claims; this is to say that it may be taught in possibilist mode by making the claim *it is possible that there are true alien claims*. Christians, for instance might think that God's universal presence coupled with his desire that all should come to know and love him make it possible that non-Christians know some truths about God, and possible that some non-Christian religions have real truths among their claims. But they might also think it not inevitable that these things follow. Perhaps it is possible for human sin to be of such depth and pervasiveness that it can prevent any particular alien religion (or even all of them) from knowing or teaching any truths about God, or indeed any religious truths at all. If this line of argument is followed, it will then be an empirical question (one that requires study of the particular facts of the case) whether some particular (or indeed any) alien religious community teaches any truths. On this possibilist view, what can be known independently of empirical study is not that there *are* true alien claims, but only that there *might be*.

Whether a particular inclusivist religion teaches that there must be or that there might be true alien claims will, then, depend upon features internal to that religion. Assessment of the plausibility of any particular version of inclusivism will therefore depend upon assessment of those features. Such features are likely to include such things as claims about the nature of God, of Buddha, of the Qur'an, or of some such. Objections to any particular inclusivist response to the question of truth (a response, recall, likely to be attractive to religious people rather than nonreligious ones) are then likely to include or require objections to the other features of the religious account from which the inclusivist response flows.

A final distinction, further analyzing inclusivism into kinds, now needs some discussion. It is the distinction, already mentioned, between closed and open inclusivism. Inclusivism is closed if it claims that all alien religious truths (should there be any) are already known to and explicitly taught by the home religion in some form. It is open if it permits the possibility that some of the truths not (yet) explicitly taught or understood by the home religion might be known to and taught by some alien religion.

Decisions about which variety of inclusivism to espouse will depend, as before, on other features of the religious account in question. But it is important to see that the decision whether to adopt closed or open inclusivism has an immediate and profound practical implication. A religion that adopts closed inclusivism decides that it has nothing to learn of significance for its own religious purposes from any alien religion. This is so because closed inclusivism includes the view that any truth taught by an alien community is already taught by the home community. Therefore, nothing new can be learned by studying and coming to know what it is that any particular alien religion teaches. Any truth that might be discovered in that way is already known to the home community. The impulse to study the particulars of what alien religions teach will therefore not be encouraged and may be seriously called into question if closed inclusivism is adopted.

Open inclusivism, by contrast, asserts at least the possibility that truths taught by alien religions might not (yet) be explicitly known to or taught by the home community. (The necessity of this state of affairs may also be taught by change of mode, as already described.) If this line is taken, and if one accepts the common-sense claim that religions are likely to want to maximize the stock of true religious claims they know and teach, a strong impetus will be provided toward coming to know the particulars of what alien religions teach; for the home religion may have something important to learn from other religions.

Actual religions, even those quite explicit about their adherence to inclusivism, are often not clear about whether they espouse open or closed inclusivism. An example of this lack of clarity will be helpful here, both to show more clearly the inner logic of inclusivism, and to provide an opportunity for an argument about the virtues of open inclusivism for Christians.

## 2.9   A Catholic Christian Argument for Open Inclusivism

The Roman Catholic Church has a long history of thinking about and responding to alien religions and alien religious claims. Much of what the Church has taught on these matters down the centuries has dealt with the question of salvation (what's to be said about the eternal destiny of those who are not Catholic Christians?), or with the question of how best to encourage those who are not Catholic Christians to become so. These questions are not the topic of this chapter; but the question of the possibility that there might be truth in alien claims has also been addressed, even if often only in passing, as a marginal comment on the other topics mentioned.

The main thrust of Church teaching on the question of truth has always been inclusivistic, which is to say that the possibility (and sometimes also the actuality) of there being such truths has always been recognized. This recognition has also typically been held together with a recognition of the inevitability (and so also the actuality) of the presence of massive and damaging error in alien religious teachings; and the latter was very often emphasized at the expense of the former. But in the twentieth century, and especially since the papacy of John XXIII (1958–63) and the Second Vatican Council (1962–5), at which important new formulations of the Church's teaching were arrived at, greater emphasis has been placed on the extent and importance of alien truth.

One of the documents promulgated at the Second Vatican Council, for example, says:

> The Catholic Church rejects nothing of what is true and holy in these [alien] religions. She considers with sincere regard those modes of living and teaching, those precepts and doctrines, which, even though they differ in many ways from those she herself holds and propounds, nonetheless often reflect a ray of the Truth that illuminates everyone.[18]

The Church here declares it not only a possibility but a fact that alien religions teach truths; it mentions, too, one reason why this is so – alien religions, like the Church, are illuminated by the triune God ("the Truth"), and it is because of this that they can and do teach what is true. The Church's detailed reasons for making this claim about alien religions and the presence of truth outside the bounds of the Church are developed elsewhere in the Council's documents, and in subsequent teachings (including some given by John Paul II, Pope at the time of my writing). A full exposition of these reasons is not possible here, but it must be noted that they include the views that all people are created by God, have their proper end in God, and are continuously given the gift of God's grace because of God's passion for their salvation. All are also subject to, and at least inchoately aware of, the moral law that governs and orders all human action. These facts, as the Church understands them to be, are what make it possible for people who explicitly know nothing of Christ or the Church, or who have rejected Christ and the Church, nonetheless to know and teach religiously significant truths.

The Church's affirmation that alien religions teach truth is, of course, through-and-through inclusivistic. That is, all such alien truth is in some way or another inferior to the Church's truths. The truths taught by alien religions are preparatory to, incomplete versions of, or useful supplements to, the truths taught by the Church. This is because the fullness of religious truth is found in Christ, and is, in the end, always about the God who is fully present in Jesus of Nazareth. And about this God the Church has been entrusted with more truth than has any alien religion – or so the Church teaches. This inclusivism is, then, very far from the parity-views discussed earlier in this chapter.

The movement of the Church's thought from general teachings about matters of fundamental concern to it (God, Christ, the nature and proper end of humans) to teaching inclusivism with respect to truth is typical, and will be evident in all religions that teach inclusivism. A full critique of or engagement with any particular religion's teaching of inclusivism (including the Catholic Christian one under discussion here) will rapidly extend into a discussion of the merits of the more central and general commitments from which it derives.

The Catholic Church, then, teaches inclusivism with respect to the question of truth, and does so for the reasons sketchily given. But does she teach open or closed inclusivism? Does she, that is, teach that there are alien truths she does not (yet) herself explicitly teach or understand, and from which she might learn? This would be open inclusivism. Or does she teach that all alien truths are already taught by her? To do so would be closed inclusivism.

The answer to this question is not clear, either in the documents of the Second Vatican Council or in subsequent Church teachings. But before saying more about this, it is important to note that the possibility of an open inclusivism can only arise for religions that do not think of themselves as already explicitly teaching all religious truth. Any religion that thought of itself as already having said all there is to be said religiously speaking, could think of alien truths only as repetitions of what it already says. If such a religion taught inclusivism, it could teach only closed inclusivism.

The Church, however, does not think of herself as already explicitly teaching all religious truth; she has not, to put it a bit more theologically, given explicit formulation to all the religiously significant truths implied by the revelation she preserves and transmits. On at least one widely held view of the development of Church teaching, giving explicit formulation to what is as yet implicit is just what the Church always does when she teaches something she has not explicitly taught before. Notice that to say of the Church that she has not given explicit formulation to all religiously significant truth is by no means to say that what she does explicitly teach is inadequate for salvation. It is only to say that there is more yet to be said, and that changing circumstances often require the saying of things not previously called for, even if implied by what is already taught.

It is, then, the fact that the Catholic Church does not think of herself as explicitly teaching all religious truth that makes both open and closed inclusivism a possibility for her. But which does she in fact teach? The answer is not clear; so far as I can tell, there is, at the end of the twentieth century no explicit teaching on the matter. So I'll now provide some suggestions about what the Church ought to teach on this question.

I begin by reiterating the claim that the Church has not yet given explicit formulation to all the religiously significant truths implied by the revelation she preserves and transmits. I add to this the almost equally uncontroversial claim that the Church may be prompted to formulate and teach what it has not previously formulated and taught by coming to know of truths discovered and taught by those outside its boundaries. Instances may be found, perhaps, in the Church's appropriation and use of work by scientists (on the size and nature of the cosmos), political theorists (on the value of democracy), and (more dubiously) economists (on the importance of the free flow of trade goods). Such truths are not always of obvious or direct religious or salvific significance; but they may nonetheless be incorporated into the Church's teachings, being baptized, of course, in the process. Something of this is evident in the development of Catholic social teaching over the last half-century. Truths so baptized, insofar as they are of religious significance, should not be thought of as extrinsic to, or not already implied by, the deposit of faith. It is part of Catholic orthodoxy to think that the deposit of faith contains implicitly everything of religious significance; but this is compatible with the claim that the Church may learn what some of these implications are from those outside its boundaries.

These facts strongly suggest that the burden of proof lies upon those who would defend closed inclusivism rather than upon those who advocate open inclusivism. That is, since the Church already acknowledges that she needs to learn some of what she must teach from those outside her boundaries, and that alien religions teach truths, there would need to be pressing reasons to deny that some of what the Church needs to learn is already to be found among the teachings of alien religions – which is precisely open inclusivism. And, so far as I can tell, there are no such reasons. It therefore follows that the Church might adopt open inclusivism as her working hypothesis for response to the question of truth raised by religious diversity, and that with such adoption ought also to become more interested than she currently is in what alien religions actually teach.

I suggest, then, that the Church ought to adopt a properly modalized open inclusivism, of the following form: *It is possible that alien religions teach truths of religious significance to the Church*; and that some of these are not yet explicitly taught or understood by the Church. Notice the difference between this and the unmodalized claim: *Alien religions do teach truths of religious significance to the Church*. This latter claim is too strong; whether there are any alien claims of the sort mentioned in a matter that should await investigation.

The too-brief argument just given has been meant to be of use in at least two ways.

First, for the non-Christian (including the nonreligious) the argument is an instance of the way in which religion-specific argument about the question of truth in the context of religious diversity is likely to go. The broadly logical features of the argument (though not of course its particulars) here given are to be found also in Buddhist and Hindu discussions of this matter (and probably also in Islamic and Jewish ones). Seeing how the argument goes should help the nonreligious to understand the patterns of thought likely to please religious people on the question.

Second, for Christians (and not just Catholic Christians) the argument is intended to recommend open inclusivism (in its properly modalized form) as the correct position. Among all the views discussed in this chapter, this is the best for Christians. Parity-views are impossible for Christians because of fundamental and axiomatically particularist claims about the significance of God's actions in Jesus of Nazareth; exclusivism cannot coherently be held by Christians because (at the very least) it contradicts the basically Christian view that the God of Abraham, Isaac, and Jacob is also the God of Jesus the Christ; and so some variety of inclusivism is the only possibility for Christians. There are interesting arguments (about the nature of grace and of human persons) to be had among Christians about whether open or closed inclusivism is to be preferred; but this book is no place to have them.

This book is also no place for arguments about whether the fundamental commitments of Christianity are true. But it can at least be said that if they are, then inclusivism (preferably open inclusivism) is not only the right answer for Christians to the question of truth in the context of religious diversity, but also the right answer simpliciter.

The nonreligious will have a harder time than the religious, philosophically speaking, with the questions of this chapter. They will be attracted, as we've seen, to one variety or another of the parity-views, and will have to deal with the difficulties, already mentioned, that beset those views. Just as legislative religious neutrality is an effective impossibility, so also philosophical neutrality with respect to the diversity of claims to religious truth is an impossibility. Philosophers here, as in so many cases, would find their intellectual life more philosophically productive were they religiously committed.

## NOTES

1   See William S. Christian, Sr., *Doctrines of Religious Communities: A Philosophical Study* (New Haven: Yale University Press, 1987).

2 I choose this example from Augustine's list of superstitions in *De doctrina christiana* [Teaching Christianity], ii.31, trans. Edmund Hill *Teaching Christianity* (Hyde Park, NY: New City Press, 1996), p. 145.

3 Henry James, *Portrait of a Lady*, in James, *Novels 1881–1886* (New York: Literary Classics of the United States, 1985), p. 324.

4 This work is translated by A. C. Senape McDermott, *An Eleventh-Century Buddhist Logic of "Exists"* (Dordrecht: Reidel, 1970).

5 Surah 112, trans. N. J. Dawood, *The Koran* (New York: Penguin, 1986), p. 265.

6 Immanuel Kant, *Religion innerhalb der Grenzen der blossen Vernunft* [Religion Within the Bounds of Reason Alone] (1793), trans. Allen W. Wood and George di Giovanni in Kant, *Religion and Rational Theology* (Cambridge: Cambridge University Press, 1996), pp. 39–215, at pp. 136–7.

7 Kant, *Religion*, p. 153.

8 Ibid.

9 John Hick, "On Conflicting Religious Truth-Claims," in Hick, *Problems of Religious Pluralism* (New York: St. Martin's Press, 1985), pp. 88–95, at p. 89.

10 Hick, "Conflicting," p. 90.

11 Ibid.

12 Ibid., p. 92.

13 Ibid., p. 95.

14 Ibid., pp. 93–4.

15 Ludwig Wittgenstein, *Lectures and Conversations on Aesthetics, Psychology and Religious Belief*, ed. Cyril Barrett (Berkeley: University of California Press, 1966), p. 53.

16 Ibid., *Lectures*, pp. 57–9.

17 Brief summaries of all these cases may be found in Carl H. Esbeck, "Table of United States Supreme Court Decisions Relating to Religious Liberty 1789–1994," *Journal of Law and Religion* 10 (1994), pp. 573–88.

18 *Nostra Aetate* §2,2, translated from the Latin given in Miikka Ruokanen, *The Catholic Doctrine of Non-Christian Religions According to the Second Vatican Council* (Leiden: Brill, 1992), p. 59.

# CHAPTER 3

# *Religious Diversity and Epistemic Confidence*

## 3.1 Epistemic Confidence

Religious diversity raises some questions about the epistemic confidence with which religious people do and should treat the assents they understand to be required of them by belonging to their religion. But what is epistemic confidence? The adjective "epistemic" means "having to do with knowledge." Roughly speaking, then, if you have epistemic confidence in an assent you make, you think that in making it you've come to know something. Every time you assent to a claim, you take the claim to be true: this is what it means to assent to a claim. But there's always the further question of what degree of trust you place in your own acts of assent, what confidence you have in the further claim *my assent to this claim yields knowledge*.

Clearly, the fact that you think some claim is true won't usually be enough by itself to give you epistemic confidence in your assent to it. Suppose you assent to (take as true) the claim *I'm the best linguist in Chicago*, and then someone tells you that your assent to this claim hasn't been formed in the right way. Perhaps you found yourself assenting to the claim as a result of consulting the tea-leaves in the bottom of your teacup; or perhaps you had a dream about the matter that left you with the assent in question. And, says your challenging interlocutor, these surely aren't the best ways to form assents about such matters as who's the best linguist in Chicago. After all, she may say, there's a Chicago Linguists' Association where all the best linguists gather every Monday night. Oughtn't you to go there and assess your skills in relation to that group before you form any opinion about whether you're the best linguist in Chicago?

Faced with such a challenge you may well find your epistemic confidence in the claim *I'm the best linguist in Chicago* significantly reduced. You may still assent to the claim (perhaps the pattern of tea-leaves was very clear or the dream very convincing), but you may find yourself beginning to have less confidence that your assent is bringing you knowledge – which is to say that your epistemic confidence in your assent may be significantly reduced. In an extreme case you may cease to assent to the claim altogether, in which case your epistemic confidence is reduced to zero.

Examples like this suggest that epistemic confidence is one aspect of your attitudes to your assents. It is a matter of degree: in some of your assents you have great epistemic confidence, in others a moderate degree, and in yet others rather little. It is possible, though psychologically complex, still to assent to a claim while yet having rather little epistemic confidence in it. This would be to find yourself involuntarily taking a claim as true while simultaneously not being very confident that it is in fact true. Suppose, for instance, you find yourself assenting to the claim *I'm fundamentally a truthful person*. This claim is part of your picture of yourself, so when you propose it to yourself or find it coming up in discussion, you assent to it (involuntarily, of course, as with all assents). And this means that you find yourself denying its contradictory when it comes up. But then a friend you trust takes you aside one day for a serious talk; she points out that you have a problem with deceit, that far too much of what you say is untrue and is known to you to be untrue when you say it, that this hurts those close to you, and that you need to make some effort to correct the problem. You protest that this isn't right, that you're a fundamentally truthful person, and that the occasional lie passing your lips is just that – occasional – and is of small significance in the context of your habitual truth-telling. Your friend tells you that you're self-deceived about this matter, that your view of yourself as fundamentally truthful is a product of wishful thinking. She asks you to keep a log for the next month of every occasion upon which you've lied, and at the end of that time to reassess the question. This conversation does not make you cease to assent to the claim *I'm fundamentally a truthful person*. You still take it to be true. But a doubt has been raised. Your epistemic confidence in your assent has been reduced, perhaps drastically if you trust the judgments and respect the motives of the friend with whom you had this conversation. You may find yourself in the position of assenting to the claim in question (of taking it as true) while yet having very little epistemic confidence in your assent.

Epistemic confidence, then, comes in degrees. It is also something that rarely comes to consciousness or gets called into question. For the vast

majority of the assents you make, religious and other, you don't consider
with what degree of epistemic confidence you make them. This question
becomes explicit, typically, in a situation of challenge, a situation like that
just described when something in your situation calls into question an
assent you make, and in so doing reduces your level of epistemic confidence in it. Ordinarily, the challenge will have to do with the pattern of
events that led up to or produced your assent. It will suggest some problem
or impropriety with that pattern, claiming, perhaps, that forming assents
in that way usually results in assenting to claims that are false. Suppose,
for instance, that as a result of consulting a (very) out-of-date almanac you
find yourself assenting to the claim *India is now part of the British Empire*.
Your challenger tells you that forming beliefs about the political order of
the world in that way – by consulting an almanac more than fifty years
out of date – is an extremely unreliable way of forming assents, that it
will often (perhaps usually) lead those who engage in it to assent to false
claims. Your challenger, let's suppose, says nothing about whether India is
now (in the year 2000) part of the British Empire; he tells you only that
you've come to believe that it is by using an unreliable method. This may
lead you to re-examine both the particular assent in question and your
habit of coming to form beliefs in this way.

It's important to notice that not all acts of assent will be produced by
the same kinds of event. For example, I assent (with a high degree of
epistemic confidence) to the claim *the computer I'm using now is three years
old*. The pattern of events that caused me to make this assent is not of the
same kind as the pattern that caused me to assent to *God spoke to Abraham*.
My computer-belief is caused (produced) by some combination of
memory-events (I recall taking delivery of a computer three years ago),
visual and tactile input (I see and feel a computer in front of me), and
judgment (I judge the computer I see and feel to be the one I took delivery of three years ago). My coming to know that any one of
these elements may not in fact have been present in the pattern of events
that produced the assent is likely to reduce my epistemic confidence
in it: perhaps I come to suspect that someone has replaced the computer
I took delivery of three years ago with a replica. My assent to the claim
about God and Abraham, by contrast, is produced by a pattern of
events of a very different kind, though saying just what the pattern is and
what kinds of event it comprises will likely be controversial. A possible
account is that I assent to that claim as a result of having read it in a book
(the Bible) that I judge to contain only truths. This is a different kind of
event than those that gave rise to my computer-belief, and that this is so

indicates the importance, when asking questions about epistemic confidence, of assessing what kinds of event ought to produce what kinds of assent.

Naturally, if you don't think of the Bible as a book that contains only truths you also likely won't think that my having read therein about God speaking to Abraham is the kind of event that obviously ought to produce assent to any claims at all – about God, about Abraham, about their relations, or indeed about anything else. Also, if you think that my memory is almost always unreliable, you likely won't think that the fact that I seem to myself to recall having taken delivery of a computer three years ago is the kind of event that ought to contribute causally to my assent to the computer-claim.

Such disagreement is most commonly and most fundamentally disagreement about what there is in the universe and what it is like – disagreement, that is, about what philosophers call ontology rather than what they call epistemology. There are, for instance, those who think that the Qur'an contains only truths and those who think that this is false. This disagreement will lead to disagreement about the degree of epistemic confidence that ought be placed in assents produced in a certain way – in this case, those formed by attentive reading of the Qur'an by those who believe that it contains only truths. There are those who think that human beings have some natural insight into moral truth, and those who think that human beings are incapable of coming to know any moral truths unless aided by a direct revelation from God. This disagreement will lead to disagreement about the degree of epistemic confidence that ought be had, for example, in assents to claims about what it's proper to do that have been formed without revelatory aid. And so on.

A particular version of such disagreement (the one that will be of most interest to this chapter) is disagreement about what ought to reduce or remove epistemic confidence in an assent already in place. This disagreement will, like those mentioned in the preceding paragraph, rest upon ontological disagreements, disagreements about what there is in the world and what it is like.

Epistemic confidence is, then, a subjective matter: it's a question of how your assents seem to you, not a question of how they actually are. This means that the central questions of this chapter are two (or perhaps better, one with a double aspect). First, descriptively, does coming to know of religious diversity typically reduce or remove religious people's epistemic confidence in the religious assents they find themselves making? Second, normatively, under what conditions is it reasonable to think that it should?

Notice that the question about epistemic confidence as just posed requires not only that there be religious diversity (specifically, diversity of religious assent), but that this fact be known. It is possible that the sheer fact of diversity might in some way reduce the warrant or justification for a particular assent even when those who make the assent in question have no idea that there is such diversity, just as those who form beliefs about their distance from objects they see in their cars' side-view mirrors without knowing that objects so seen are always closer than they appear are likely to form false beliefs about the matter without knowing that they are doing so. But their epistemic confidence in the assents they do come to make will not be reduced or removed unless they come to know the relevant facts about side-view mirrors. Similarly, those who don't know about diversity of religious assent can't have their epistemic confidence in their assents reduced or removed by it. I'll restrict my attention to the question of whether awareness of diversity does or should reduce or remove epistemic confidence partly because that's where most of the contemporary discussion is focussed, and partly because religious people do, sometimes, seem to be troubled, cognitively, by coming to know of religious diversity.

## 3.2   Awareness of Diversity

Awareness of diversity in belief and action has deeply different effects upon different people in different contexts. Sometimes it significantly reduces epistemic confidence in particular assents, even to the point of removing it altogether; and sometimes such knowledge has no effect at all upon epistemic confidence. It will be helpful to look at some differences of this sort in order to understand better some common trajectories of thought on the matter.

Consider a professional economist, someone who has devoted her career to studying the economic effects of minimum-wage legislation. She has published widely on the matter and has a high national profile as an advocate of the view that legislative attempts to raise the minimum wage have negative effects upon those who do the jobs for which such wages are paid. Perhaps she argues that such legislation reduces the number of such jobs, or makes their geographic distribution uneven. Since she's a professional economist she knows that there are other economists, with qualifications and a track record at least the equal of hers, who hold utterly incompatible views about the effects of minimum-wage legislation (there is no interesting issue in economics of which this is untrue). She is aware, that is, of diversity of assent on the matter at hand. But such knowledge is unlikely to reduce her epistemic confidence in the beliefs she has about the effects of minimum-wage legislation. It is much more likely that she will judge those who have beliefs on the matter incompatible with hers, and who advocate legislation incompatible with the legislation she advocates, to be mistaken. They have, from her point of view, come to make the assents they make in the wrong way. Perhaps, in her view, they have misread the evidence because they are blinded by political ideology; or perhaps they seem to her too stupid properly to assess the evidence. In either case, something has, it seems to her, gone wrong with the pattern of events that produced their assents, and she is therefore unlikely to find her own epistemic confidence reduced or removed by having her nose rubbed in the fact of continuing diversity of belief about minimum-wage legislation.

Imagine a different case. Someone is convinced that a certain kind of crystal has healing powers. He meditates before a specimen of this crystal daily, and is convinced that doing so has removed his arthritis and brought him tranquility. He also knows that many (perhaps most) people do not share his beliefs about the efficacy of crystals, and that the majority of the medical profession would reject them out of hand as both false and improperly formed. Although his knowledge that there is deep diversity of belief on this matter does not immediately lead him to cease to assent to the crystal-claims he values, nor in his own mind to have less epistemic confidence in them, it does lead him to reconstrue these assents in a gradual and subtle way. He comes to see them as assents in which he does and should have epistemic confidence, but not as assents everyone should make. If he has some philosophical interests and sophistication he may come to think that the claim he assents to about the crystals is not *crystals heal*, but rather, *for me, assenting to "crystals heal" heals*. If he has no philosophical interests he may simply say that what he believes about crystals is true for him, that he has a perfect right to assent to it with a high degree of epistemic confidence. These moves reconfigure the crystal-claim; they turn it from a claim primarily about an aspect of the setting of human life relevant to all into a claim primarily about a particular believer. The crystal-believer has, partly under the pressure of becoming aware of diversity in crystal-beliefs, privatized his act of assent, and in so doing turned its object into a claim whose scope and demand are limited to himself (and perhaps to those who share his idiosyncrasies).

A third example. As an immigrant to the United States, and thus not well versed in that country's geography, I for some time was of the opinion that Kansas City is to be found in the state of Kansas. This seems, on the face of it, not an unreasonable thing to think; and so far as I thought about my assent to this claim and the degree of epistemic confidence I had in it, it seemed to me that I both had and should have a high degree of such confidence – about as much, perhaps, as in my assent to the claim *Mexico City is in Mexico*. But one day, asking a new acquaintance where she was from, I got the answer "Kansas City, Missouri." I expressed my surprise, and had it explained to me that most of Kansas City is in fact in Missouri. In this way, my epistemic confidence in my assent to the claim *Kansas City is in Kansas* was severely reduced, and upon checking the atlas, I ceased to assent to that claim. I came to do so largely because of epistemic pressure brought to bear by coming to know of diversity of belief about the question of Kansas City's location. I found myself in a minority of one about the question, in fact; I judged that the pattern of events that produced my earlier assent (a simple inference from similarity of name to similarity of location) was not in this case reliable; and I further judged my new sources (the acquaintance from Missouri, as well as the atlas) to be trustworthy and authoritative. In this case, then, coming to know of diversity of assent caused me drastically to reduce my epistemic confidence in an assent of mine, and eventually to cease to make it.

These cases are intended to illustrate the variety of ways in which knowledge of diversity may affect epistemic confidence. They're intended to be typical, and to point to two of the key variables that affect the ways in which people respond to their coming to know that others have beliefs on some matter which are incompatible with their own. The first of these is the degree of epistemic confidence with which the initial assent is made. If the initial assent bears a very high degree of epistemic confidence (as in the case of the economist), then she is, to a corresponding degree, unlikely to find her confidence in her assent significantly decreased simply by her coming to know that others not only do not make the same assent, but assent to claims incompatible with the claim to which she assents. There will, then, be a relation of inverse proportionality between the strength of the initial epistemic confidence and the extent to which it is reduced by the simple knowledge of diversity.

The second variable is the degree to which those making (and perhaps advocating) incompatible assents seem trustworthy and authoritative to those who know or come to know of them. In the case of the crystal-believer, perhaps the fact that all or most of those who know (or ought to know) about healing do not believe that crystals heal has more effect by way of reducing epistemic confidence than would be the case if those who held or advocated contrary beliefs were all fast-food workers, and so without apparent authority on such questions. And in the case of my mistake about Kansas City, those propounding the contradictory view seemed to me very trustworthy and eminently authoritative.

Descriptively, then, knowledge of diversity will typically reduce epistemic confidence most not only when those holding and advocating incompatible beliefs seem authoritative and trustworthy, but also when the initial assent bears low epistemic confidence for the one who makes it. When one or both of these factors is absent, knowledge of diversity of belief about some topic may not reduce epistemic confidence at all.

So far, what I've said has been largely descriptive. It has been intended to capture something of the range of ways in which people actually do respond to the knowledge of diversity. Is it also possible to say more, to say how we ought respond to knowledge of diversity, rather than just how we do? Here I suggest that we ought to place a good deal of confidence in the way people really do respond to their coming to know about diversity of assent on some matter. This is not least because we have no other real option: How else could we in fact respond? But it is also because if we transpose the descriptive claims made in the last few paragraphs into a normative key, they remain entirely reasonable as a description of how we should go about managing our assents. If you have high epistemic confidence in your initial assent to some claim – perhaps because it seems to you (if you're forced to consider the matter) that the pattern of events that preceded, underlay, and in part caused you to make the assent in question is just the right pattern, the pattern that's reliable in producing assents in all matters of this sort (whatever this sort is) – then coming to know that some people make incompatible assents ought not, by itself, reduce your epistemic confidence. If, however, those who make assents incompatible with yours are, from your perspective, authoritative and trustworthy on the matter in question, then this should (as it typically will) reduce your epistemic confidence in your assent. And if both factors are in place (strong initial confidence, challenge by the authoritative), you'll then be (and should be) in a situation of some epistemic difficulty: it will not be obvious what will or should happen to your level of epistemic confidence. No single or simple algorithm will tell you just what to do in such a case.

Certain sorts of assent, however, carry with them a kind of codicil or rider. They imply that any normally-equipped human being in the situation you're now in will assent to what you now assent to. Suppose you're looking out of the window and you see that it's raining. Your assent to *it's raining now* comes with the assumption just mentioned: you'd expect any normally-equipped person in your situation to have just this belief. Another way of putting this is to say that for assents of this kind all normally-equipped humans are authoritative. You'll be puzzled if, when your friend comes into the room and looks out of the window, she doesn't come to assent to *it's raining now*. You'll probably respond by trying to find out what's wrong with her eyes or her mind. But if you gather a group of friends and you're the only one who assents to *it's raining now* upon looking out of the window, you're likely to respond by trying to find out what's wrong with yourself – and properly so. For with assents of this kind – assents for which all normally-equipped humans are authoritative – the degree of challenge to epistemic confidence produced by coming to know of diversity of assent is likely to be (and should be) directly proportional to the number of those who have beliefs incompatible with yours.

But many assents are not of this sort, which is to say that not all humans are equally authoritative with respect to them. Many assents can only be made after special training has been given and local knowledge thereby gained. Coming to know that those without this special training and local knowledge make assents incompatible with yours on some matter to which such training and such knowledge are relevant neither is nor should be in the least epistemically troubling. Suppose I take an English friend to her first baseball game; after the third strike is called on Henry she has the belief *Henry's still in* while I have the belief *Henry's out*. But she assents to *Henry's still in* only because she doesn't understand baseball; the fact that she assents to this claim doesn't reduce my epistemic confidence in *Henry's out* in the least. You don't come to have the right beliefs about baseball merely by being human and finding yourself at a game; you need special training and local knowledge to know what's going on. And this is to say that not everyone is or ought to be equally epistemically authoritative with respect to assents about matters of baseball.

In cases where an assent can only properly be made if someone is correctly trained to make it, explanations for diversity of assent are easily had. Those who don't believe what they ought in economics, baseball, mathematics (or religion) are, it might be said, ignorant, blinded by passion, or subject to sin – and these are the reasons why they get it wrong. Where such explanations are available, their use will be one of the things that permits those faced with diversity of belief not to find their epistemic confidence in their assents to be thereby reduced or removed. Our economist isn't troubled by diversity of belief about the effects of minimum-wage legislation because she can explain it by ignorance (on the part of those untrained in economics), or ideological passion (on the part of those trained but disagreeing). Diversity of assent will become more epistemically troubling to the extent that explanations for it fail – and so our economist may find herself challenged epistemically by disagreement on the part of those trained in economics who share her political commitments in ways that she would not be by those trained in economics who occupy a different place in the political spectrum. And this is the third variable that typically (and properly) affects the way in which knowledge of diversity changes epistemic confidence.

A proper response to the question of epistemic confidence raised by knowledge of diversity then should take into account three variables. First, the strength of the epistemic confidence possessed by the initial assent; second, the perceived trustworthiness or authoritativeness of those who make and advocate incompatible assents; and third, as I've just shown, the extent to which the fact of diversity is explicable (predictable, comprehensible when encountered) on the initial assents. What then is to be said about religious assents and acceptances (those required or suggested by inhabiting a religion) with respect to these variables in the light of knowledge of diversity in religious assents?

### 3.3   Religious Responses to the Question of Epistemic Confidence

There is no single and unavoidable answer to the question of how inhabitants of a religious form of life ought to respond, epistemically speaking, to their coming to know of irreducible diversity in religious assent. The response given by any particular religious person will naturally and properly depend upon the specifics of the religious account of things from within which the response is made, and since these particulars vary greatly, so too will (and should) the responses. Some religions, for example, may not predict diversity of religious assents and might therefore neither offer nor be able to offer an explanation of its occurrence when encountered. Others may have strong reasons for denying trustworthiness or authoritativeness to those who advocate or present alien beliefs and practices.

Inhabitants of religions of these two kinds will naturally vary as to the epistemic trouble given them by their coming to know of diversity in religious assent.

There are, though, some predictable common factors in the epistemic responses of the religiously committed when they come to know of diversity in religious assent. Most obviously, there is the fact that, on the understanding of religion in play in this book, it is likely that the acts of assent and acceptance associated with inhabiting any particular religion will be made with a very high degree of epistemic confidence. It is typical that religious people understand their religious assents to be made with more epistemic confidence than any other assents they make (or at least that they would so understand them were the question to be pressed – most religious people, quite properly, don't think explicitly about the degree of epistemic confidence with which their assents are made). This is because one of the features of a religious form of life is that it seems unsurpassable to those who inhabit it; at the cognitive level this feature will frequently make itself felt as the non-negotiability and unquestionability of the assents of central importance to the religion. To say that an assent seems to someone at a particular time to be unquestionable or non-negotiable is precisely to say that it seems to them to be made with a very high (perhaps maximal) degree of epistemic confidence at that time. And if you make an act of assent that seems to you of this sort, you will likely be relatively untroubled epistemically by your coming to know that others make assents to claims incompatible with yours.

If you examine the web of claims to which you assent you'll find that some of them seem to you beyond question. Some of them lie sufficiently close to the center of your belief-web that abandoning them, it will seem to you, would require a drastic and comprehensive reweaving of the web. This will be true whether or not you offer a religious account of things. You are likely, for instance, to have beliefs about your own past of this sort: that you were born to these parents, attended that school, are a citizen of such-and-such a country, and so on. You do not seriously consider, probably, whether to cease to assent to these claims; and if someone calls them into question you are unlikely to devote much time or effort to considering whether your challenger is right or wrong. Since it is perfectly obvious to you that you are right about these things, it will follow fairly directly that anyone who believes something incompatible with what you believe about them must, ipso facto, be mistaken. These assents to claims about your own past are, then, unquestionable and non-negotiable for you, and this is because they are at or close to the center of your web of belief, and their abandonment would require the web to be rewoven almost completely.

Other assents are not like this. I, for instance, assent to many claims about the dating of events in Indian history, and about the authorship of Buddhist texts. But I place little epistemic confidence in most of these, and would seriously consider challenges to them. Were I to abandon what I now hold about the likely dates of King Kaniska, for instance, this would require only minor adjustments to my belief-web, since only a few insignificant filaments at the periphery would have been thereby altered.

Religious assents, of course, are for those who make them much more like beliefs about one's parentage or one's present geographical location than like assents to claims about peripherally relevant matters of fact. My assents to claims like *God is loving me now* or *the God of Abraham and Isaac is the God of Jesus of Nazareth* are, in terms of the degree of epistemic confidence I place in them and in terms of their closeness to the center of my web of belief, very like my assents to the claims *I am married* (I am), and *my spouse is a human being* (she is). The same would be true, with appropriate changes, for a married Buddhist's assents to claims like *Buddha's compassion is unmatched.* For such a Buddhist, serious consideration of the possible truth or desirability of the denial of the claims central to her Buddhism will be (and ought to be) as odd as serious consideration of the denial of the claim *my spouse is a human being.* Coming to know that there is diversity of belief on these matters may be interesting to such a person, but is very unlikely to appear to her seriously (or at all) to reduce the epistemic confidence she places in her assents with respect to them. It will not, that is to say, give rise to serious epistemic worries for her.

This, then, is the first and most important thread in the epistemic response that religiously-committed people are likely to make upon coming to know of religious diversity. Because their religious assents are, for them, made with a very high degree of epistemic confidence, knowledge of diversity will typically not be troubling. This thread in the religious response should remind you of the Wittgensteinean understanding of religious belief discussed in chapter 2. It is one of the strengths of such an understanding that it gives proper credit to this element of being religious. But this thread in the religious response speaks only to the first of the three variables mentioned above − the strength and depth of the epistemic confidence with which the central assents are made. There is more to be said about the other two variables; attention to these in some respects calls into question the dismissal of the epistemic difficulty suggested by the first variable.

The second variable, recall, is the perceived trustworthiness or author-itativeness of those who hold and advocate alien claims, especially where these are incompatible with claims of central importance to the home religion. Consider the following scenario. A faithful Christian assents to the following claim: *Only those responding rightly to God will exhibit the gifts and fruits of the Spirit in their lives.* He also thinks that this claim is central to his religion. He is likely to understand the fruits of the Spirit (the gifts given by the Holy Spirit to the faithful) in biblical terms (Isaiah 11:2, Galatians 5:22–23), and to include among them love, joy, peace, patience, kindness, goodness, generosity, gentleness, faithfulness, modesty, self-control, and chastity. Suppose further that this Christian comes to know some faithful Buddhists very well, and is forced (perhaps reluctantly) thereby to acknowledge that, so far as he can tell, these qualities are evident in their lives to a very high degree, perhaps even to a higher degree than is the case for his own life or for the lives of other Christians he knows. He is then likely to assent to the claim *these Buddhists are responding rightly to God* – for this is entailed, on his own view, by the fact that their lives exhibit the fruits of the Spirit.

This situation is not uncommon for religious people who come to know faithful religious aliens. It has certainly been mine as a Christian in coming to know faithful Jews and Buddhists moderately well. The situa-tion can weaken (or at least interestingly complicate) the usual mainte-nance by religious people of epistemic confidence in the face of knowledge of diversity. It can do this by suggesting the following pattern of argument (for Christians; parallel patterns could easily be constructed for others). The religious alien, the evidence of his life suggests, is in at least some ways responding rightly to God. Responding rightly to God involves knowledge (implicit knowledge, maybe, but still knowledge) of what God wants of humans. Those in possession of such knowledge should be taken seriously when they offer explicit teaching about the nature of human beings, the environment in which humans live, and the proper ends of human life. Therefore, the religious alien's teachings about the nature of humans and their environment should be taken seriously.

Coming to think, by way of a pattern of argument of this sort, that alien teachings ought seriously to be considered is very far from coming to think them true. It is equally far from coming to think that the teach-ings and doctrines of the home religion ought to be corrected by alien claims, or abandoned when there is a contradiction between domestic and alien claims. But it may raise the beginnings of an epistemic question, a question about the degree of confidence with which one's religious assents ought to be made. Perhaps the following thought might occur: If people who are responding rightly to God teach things about human life and what it is for that are incompatible with what we teach, perhaps we should sit a little looser to what we teach, for we now have some reason to think that these aliens are at least trustworthy and perhaps even authoritative in these matters. Of course, not all religious people need follow such a pattern of thought when they come to know that religious aliens – even those who teach what appears incompatible with the teachings of the home community – nonetheless lead lives that are (in terms of what the home community expects of its members) quite admirable. The home community might, after all, teach that good morals are compatible with bad metaphysics, and might then not be in the least troubled by the fact that morally admirable aliens offer claims of a metaphysical sort that contradict domestic claims of that same sort. This strongly suggests that whether the challenge to epistemic confidence from awareness of diversity becomes more pressing as a result of discovering that religious aliens are at least as moral as religious kin will, as always, depend upon the particulars of the home religion's account of things.

Religious people who do have epistemic questions raised (or suggested) by coming to think that religious aliens might be trustworthy or authoritative are then likely to look to their own accounts of things to see whether these can offer an explanation of the alien's possible authoritativeness. And this brings us to the third variable involved in response to the challenge posed to epistemic confidence by knowledge of religious diversity. Can the domestic account explain the fact of diversity? Does it have the resources to say both why incompatible alien accounts exist, and why there are agreements of some limited extent between alien teachings and domestic teachings? (I assume that the domestic account is not exclusivist on the question of truth, for if it were it would not permit the possibility of agreement between the domestic account and any alien account on any question whatever.) The extent to which such explanatory resources are lacking is likely to be closely linked to the extent to which the challenge posed to epistemic confidence by knowledge of diversity comes to seem pressing.

Consider, for example, the case of a religion whose teachings lead its inhabitants to expect uniformity of belief on the question of whether there is a supreme being who is worthy of worship. Suppose, further, that inhabitants of this religion come to discover that there is no such uniformity –

that there are not only nonreligious people who assent to no such claim, but also religious aliens who assent to and advocate claims incompatible with it. Such inhabitants will then usually be forced to turn back to their own religious account of things in order to see whether it has the resources to account for a state of affairs it did not predict, and to do so in the especially difficult situation of knowing that it did not predict a state of affairs which it then finds to be actual. The needed explanatory resources will often be found: religious accounts are typically internally complex and capable of being made to yield conclusions not obvious to any inhabitant of the religion until new circumstances make the need for finding them evident. But sometimes it will prove difficult or impossible to find such resources; and when this is the case, the challenge to epistemic confidence posed by knowledge of religious diversity is likely to become pressing, even to the point where assents that had been made with much confidence now seem worthy of only a little confidence even when they continue to be made.

In such cases, a particular assent or set of assents begins by being made with a high degree of epistemic confidence, as is typically the case for religious beliefs; but confidence in it is progressively and in the end irreversibly weakened by the increasing authoritativeness and trustworthiness of those who offer and advocate incompatible claims, as well as by the fact that the home religion lacks the predictive or explanatory resources to deal with the matter.

This is not the only, nor the most likely result of knowledge of diversity on the part of the religiously committed. Much more common is the maintenance of high confidence in the home religion's account of things by finding explanatory resources within that account to impugn the authoritativeness and trustworthiness of those who advocate alien and incompatible claims (the devil made them say what they say; they say what they say because of accumulated bad karma – and so on). And even in cases where an assent once made with confidence is abandoned, this is unlikely to result in the abandonment of the entire religious account of which that particular assent formed a small part.

To summarize this section. The response of those with religious commitments to the challenge that knowledge of diversity provides to epistemic confidence will depend upon the particulars of their commitments. For some (perhaps most), knowledge of diversity will not be especially troubling, epistemically speaking: if their initial religious assents are made with a good deal of confidence, and if they can explain diversity by appeal to the particulars of their account (perhaps by calling into question the trustworthiness of those who advocate alien claims), then they will not be epistemically disturbed by their coming to know of diversity. But the extent to which any of these things is not the case is precisely the extent to which the challenge to epistemic confidence posed by coming to know of diversity will seem serious, and may lead to the abandonment or reconstrual of some elements of the domestic account – or even, in the extreme case, to the abandonment of the entire account.

There is, however, a particular kind of response to the epistemic challenge posed by knowledge of diversity that has become increasingly common in the democracies of Europe and the Americas over the last two centuries or so, and that is paradoxically held in common by some of those who call themselves religious and some of those who do not. Because of its prevalence, and because it has some philosophical interest, it deserves separate treatment.

## 3.4 Privatization

In April of 1992 the United States Supreme Court heard arguments in a suit brought by Planned Parenthood (and others) against the State of Pennsylvania in the person of its then-governor Robert P. Casey (I'll call this case *Casey* from here on). The suit was a challenge to the constitutionality of some Pennsylvania laws regulating the conditions under which abortions could be carried out in that state. The laws in question required, among other things, that a married woman seeking an abortion should sign a statement saying that she had notified her husband of her intention to abort; and that she could not have an abortion until she had been provided by the state with information about the procedure and its implications at least 24 hours prior to the planned abortion, and had indicated that she understood this material.

The challenge to the constitutionality of these laws was brought in large part on the basis of earlier Supreme Court decisions about the constitutional basis for a woman's right to choose abortion without excessive interference from the state. These earlier decisions had located the right in question in the due process clause of the Fourteenth Amendment, which says that no state shall "deprive any person of life, liberty, or property, without due process of law." The Court had read the liberty component of this clause to guarantee at least all the substantive liberties mentioned in the Bill of Rights (freedom of speech, of religion, of assembly, and so forth), but also to mark out several spheres of human activity into which the propriety of any state intrusion would be severely limited by the Constitution. These spheres of activity included matters to do with the family (marriage) and with reproduction (contraception); but they also included, most interestingly for our purposes, the sphere of belief–formation about matters of deep or broad importance to those forming the beliefs.

On the liberty to form such beliefs without undue interference by the state, the Court's majority opinion had this to say:

> At the heart of liberty is the right to define one's own concept of exis-
> tence, of meaning, of the universe, and of the mystery of human life. Beliefs
> about these matters could not define the attributes of personhood were they
> formed under compulsion of the State.[1]

There's much of interest in this brief passage, as there also is in the majority opinion of which it forms a part, as well as in the dissenting opinions
(the Court's majority opinion ruled, among other things, the 24-hour
waiting period requirement constitutional and the spousal-information
requirement not so; but there was dissent among the Justices about
those matters, as well as – more fundamentally – about whether the Due
Process Clause of the Fourteenth Amendment ought to be read to
cover a right to abortion). But my interest here is only in the notion of
an individual right to define one's own beliefs about such things as one's
"concept of existence, of meaning, of the universe, and of the mystery of
human life" – about what, in the terms of this book, are properly religious matters, matters that do (or are very likely to) form part of a comprehensive, unsurpassable, and centrally important account of things. More
specifically still, I'm interested in the epistemological implications of asserting such a right as (in part) a response to knowledge of diversity of belief
on such matters.

It's pretty clear that the Court asserts such a right in large part as a
response to its awareness that citizens of the United States do in fact hold
very widely diverse and largely incompatible beliefs about "the mystery of
human life" (from now on I'll call these religious beliefs by way of shorthand, even though the Court does not explicitly so call them in this
context). The Court's judgment in *Casey* is representative of a long and
well developed tradition of judicial reasoning in its argument that it can
be no part of the State's function (legislative or judicial) to say what the
correct views on matters of this sort are, much less to attempt to compel
assent to any particular set of such claims. Still further, as the quoted

excerpt from the opinion explicitly states, the Court thinks that religious beliefs formed under State compulsion could not function for those who had so formed them in the way that such beliefs ought; that is, they could not carry conviction or provoke assent as part of a religious account of things. They would instead become claims to be honored with the lips but not with the heart.

The Court's opinion locates religious belief firmly in the private sphere. This is the point of the appeal to the Fourteenth Amendment: religious belief is placed in a sphere of human activity about which the State can have nothing to say, positively or negatively, a sphere in which the individual is sovereign. There is a genealogical connection here with William James's understanding of religion:

> Religion . . . shall mean for us the feelings, acts, and experiences of individual men in their solitude, so far as they apprehend themselves to stand in relation to whatever they may consider the divine.[2]

For the Court, as for James, religious assent is a private matter, a matter solely within the province of the individual to determine. In this it is like a decision about whom to marry (this is another sphere of human activity protected from state interference by the Court's reading of the Fourteenth Amendment), or a decision about which baseball team to support (not mentioned by the Court as an example, but sure to be were there any state attempts to coerce it that might produce a challenge).

The idea that religious assents are private is connected with the idea that they are a matter of choice or preference. And this complex of terms (privacy-choice-preference) is deeply woven into the fabric of late twentieth-century American (and to a lesser extent European and Asian) thought about the proper formation and epistemic status of religious assents. Part of the explanation for the depth with which this complex of ideas has entered into the American soul is precisely the religious freedom provision of the First Amendment ("Congress shall make no law concerning the establishment of religion . . ."), together with the traditions of legislative and judicial action that have flowed from it. The *Casey* decision is an instance of work in these traditions; its appeal to the Fourteenth Amendment illustrates the power of the privacy-choice-preference complex of ideas as a tool of constitutional interpretation.

But these broadly constitutional matters are not the only influences upon the seeming obviousness of the idea that religious assents are a matter of individual preference. There is also the fact that the dominant economic forms of life are now and have been for almost two centuries directly predicated upon the idea that the individual preference and unfettered choice of consumers are fundamental goods, and that they ought to be restricted as little as is compatible with the existence of a democratic polity at the beginning of the twenty-first century. The ever-increasing influence of late-capitalist economic forms (the global multinational corporation is the most familiar, but international markets in currency and stocks are equally important) encourages those who live and move and have their being under the sway of these (and that means all of us except for the most strong-willed separatists, such as the Amish in their refusal of modern consumer goods, or radical antifederalist and survivalist groups in the mountains of Idaho and Montana) to understand every aspect of their lives in terms of this fundamentally economic model: as a matter of choice and preference, to be explicitly dictated by no one, though subject to persuasion by anyone. Americans and Europeans at the beginning of the new millennium are therefore likely naturally and automatically to see themselves as most basically consumers, whether of material goods (which car shall I buy?), of sexual and emotional goods (whom shall I marry? with whom shall I have sex?), of religious goods (which church shall I join?), or of cognitive goods (to which claims about the mystery of human life shall I give my assent?). All these choices will tend to be seen as of the same fundamental kind, which is to say as ideally unconstrained and private, a matter of preferential choice among a multiplicity of goods, not all of which can be chosen by any one person, but none of which ought to be ruled out for any person by state action.

So understanding choice of religious assents in a world of religious diversity has some important epistemic implications, and it's these that are most important for our investigation. The most important epistemic implications of the move to a privatized, preference-based understanding of religious assents is that all of them will easily begin to seem (even to those who make them) on a par with one another, epistemically speaking. Certainly they will be seen as on a legal par; indeed, ensuring that they are so seen is the Court's main interest in *Casey* (as it also is in many other decisions). But they may very well also come to be seen as on an epistemic par: legal rights may easily come to be translated into epistemic rights, and that such a move is often made is evident in many of our ordinary speech habits. "I've a right to my beliefs," we say – and we may often be confused as to whether we mean legal right or epistemic right, and as a result of this confusion may come to think that we mean both.

But saying that two acts of assent are epistemically on a par is to say something complicated, something that doesn't immediately follow from the Court's largely procedural interests. Using the language of this chapter, the claim of epistemic parity may mean that two acts of assent are and ought to be made with equal epistemic confidence. I assent to the claim *strawberry milkshakes taste better than chocolate ones*, you to the claim *chocolate milkshakes taste better than strawberry ones*, and we each do so with a very high degree of epistemic confidence. In this sense the two assents are on an epistemic par. But they may also reasonably be thought to be on an epistemic par because the pattern of events that produced them was, in each case, of fundamentally the same kind, and therefore not to be distinguished with respect to propriety. I was brought to make my assent by facts about my past and my physical make-up (perhaps in early childhood I was encouraged to like strawberry-tasting things better than chocolate-tasting things, or perhaps there's something about my genetic inheritance that disposes me in this direction); and you were similarly brought to make your assent. It's not that one of us was rightly brought to form our assent and the other wrongly. The fact that the claims we assent to appear incompatible at first blush (can it be the case both that strawberry shakes taste better and that chocolate ones do?) doesn't alter this judgment about epistemic parity because we can easily reinterpret the claims (by privatizing them, making my claim principally about me and your claim principally about you, rather than understanding either of them to be principally about milkshakes) so as to remove this apparent incompatibility.

For a rather different example, consider someone living in tenth-century Europe who would likely have assented to the claim *the world on which we live is flat*. I assent (as probably do you) to the claim *the world on which we live is an oblate spheroid*. These two claims are incompatible both at first blush and after long acquaintance, which is to say that they cannot both be true. They differ in this respect from the milkshake-claims considered in the preceding paragraph. But is there still a sense in which assents to them can be understood to be on an epistemic par? (They are obviously not on a par with respect to truth.) In some epistemic respects they could reasonably be thought to be on a par: perhaps I and my tenth-century counterpart make our assents with equal confidence; perhaps, too, neither of us is malfunctioning cognitively, and each of us has taken into account all the evidence that we reasonably could take into account on the matter. All the authorities you trust tell you that the earth is flat, and, moreover, it seems flat to your eyes. All the authorities I trust tell me that the earth is an oblate spheroid, and, moreover, I've seen pictures taken from space that show it to be so.

But there is at least one important respect in which the patterns of events that caused each of us to make our respective assents differ from one another. It is that the environment in which my tenth-century counterpart came to make his assent was not appropriate for coming to make assents to true claims on the question of the earth's shape (because all the authorities and evidence pointed the wrong way); by contrast, the environment in which I came to make my assent was appropriate for coming to make assents to true claims on the matter (because all the authorities and evidence pointed the right way). The problem or impropriety, then, lies not in either of the people making their assents, but rather in one of the environments in which those assents are made. Whether an impropriety of this sort should be categorized as an epistemic one depends on where you draw the boundaries around epistemology. If you think that questions about what knowledge is and how we do and ought to get it (epistemological questions, that is) have to do primarily or only with what the individual does in coming to make her assents (with whether her belief-forming mechanisms are functioning properly, with whether she has fulfilled her epistemic duties, and so on), then environmental difficulties such as the one mentioned in this example won't be primarily epistemological and it will be possible to say that the flat-earth belief and the round-earth belief are on an epistemic par. If, however, you include environmental factors in your understanding of those things that epistemology should attend to, then the difference between my environment and that of my tenth-century counterpart will be epistemically significant, and it will follow that there is at least one respect in which our beliefs are not on an epistemic par. However you understand the limits of epistemology, though, it will remain the case that what it reasonably appeared to my tenth-century counterpart that he knew and what it reasonably appears to me that I know differ with respect to their truth-value even if not with respect to anything we've each done in coming to make our assents; and that the explanation for this must lie in some problem with the environment in which we came to make our assents.

In the case of the two milkshake claims, then, apparently incompatible though they are, it's reasonable to say that they're fully on an epistemic par. There's no need to think that anyone is wrong, nor any need to postulate a problem with the pattern of events (environmental or cognitive) that caused each assent to be made. And the apparent incompatibility between them can be resolved by the elegant and deeply attractive (to those who understand choice, preference, and privacy to be the key values governing their cognitive life) solution of privatizing them, making them have to do with the people who assent to them rather than with any shared element of the human environment. Giving in to the pull toward privatization makes it possible for everyone to be right because, in the end, everyone's assents on the matters that have been privatized turn out to be assents to claims about their own preferences. This is why privatization is so attractive to the nonreligious as an answer to the question of epistemic confidence posed by knowledge of diversity. It permits all those who make religious assents to understand themselves and be understood by others as being on an epistemic par with each other; it permits them, also, to have as much epistemic confidence as they like (and in the case of my strawberry-milkshake assent that's a lot) in their religious assents, and to be happily allowed to do so even by the nonreligious. Following the pull to privatization permits all those who make religious assents to enter not only a safe legal haven, as the Court would wish, but also a safe epistemic haven, as the Court probably also wishes. On this understanding, then, becoming aware of religious diversity is and should be no more epistemically troubling for religious people than coming to know of diversity in milkshake-tastes is for milkshake-consumers.

But it is far less clear that religious people can happily take the road suggested to them by the Court. The establishment of epistemic parity among religious assents by making them expressions of preference privatizes them in the interest of protecting them from interference by the agencies of the state (which was the Court's main interest in *Casey*). But it also protects them from being taken seriously as elements in comprehensive accounts of the way things are. If I follow the pull toward privatization by interpreting your religious assent to *everyone should take refuge in the Buddha* as an assent to a preference claim (like *everyone should drive a Volkswagen*) then I'm likely not going to understand it as a claim around assent to which your entire life is organized, and I'm certainly not going to understand it as a claim around which my entire life ought to be organized. I am likely instead to think of it as an expression of refined (if exotic) taste on your part; I will probably not look for explanations of what went wrong in the events that caused you to come to make this assent; and even if I assent to claims like *Jesus of Nazareth is of unparalleled significance for everyone*, I'm not likely to think that you and I disagree in any important way (any more than I would if I thought everyone should drive a Toyota).

The tradition of judicial interpretation represented by the Supreme Court's majority opinion in *Casey* is of course not aimed directly at the epistemological questions treated in this chapter. But its attempt to demarcate a private space for religious assents, a space into which the long arm of the state cannot reach, is part of a pervasive pattern of thinking about religious assents that does have implications for these questions. It is, as we've seen, a powerfully pervasive pattern of thinking that pulls those in its thrall toward privatization, toward answering the question of epistemic confidence in the context of known diversity by claiming epistemic parity for all religious assents. This is not a route that will appeal to those who make religious assents, because they will typically look for an explanation of diversity in religious assents in terms of some impropriety in the course of events that produced assents to claims incompatible with their own; this means that they cannot rest content with a privatized, preference-model of such assents, since there is no room for epistemic error in such a model. But the cultural depth and pervasiveness of the consumerist construal of religious assents as matters of preference is now such that it is increasingly difficult for religious people in the United States or Europe to maintain an epistemologically critical response to diversity, and increasingly tempting to follow the pull toward epistemic parity suggested by privatization. To the extent that this temptation is succumbed to, though, a religious account of things effectively ceases to be offered, even where its form and rhetoric remain. It is one of the ironies of the American experiment with religious liberty that it has become implicated in these ways, causally if not intentionally, with the destruction of properly religious forms of life.

So far I've suggested that there will be differences in approach to the question about epistemic confidence posed by knowledge of diversity between the religious and the nonreligious. For the latter, knowledge of diversity will often be seen as requiring the conclusion that all religious assents are on an epistemic par. There are numerous ways to express this conclusion, but most common is the view that religious assents are an expression of preference, and can therefore safely be privatized. For the former, answers given will depend upon the extent to which the doctrines and teachings of the home community seem to its inhabitants to be assented to with confidence, the extent to which they can predict and explain the facts of religious diversity, and the extent to which religious aliens who advocate claims incompatible with those advocated by the home religion, are understood to be trustworthy and authoritative. Religions differ about each of these matters, and to see in more detail how discussion of them is likely to go, it will be useful to look in some depth at a particular instance of Christian discussion of the epistemic effects of knowledge of religious diversity.

### 3.5 The Epistemic Significance of Religious Diversity: A Christian View in Conversation with William Alston

William Alston's book *Perceiving God*, published in 1991, offers a detailed analysis from a Christian point of view of what it is to perceive God, and of what epistemic status the beliefs resulting from such perceptions have. In the course of this analysis he gives some discussion to the topic of this chapter – to the question, that is, of the epistemic significance (for religious people – or, more specifically still, for Christians) of their coming to know of diversity in religious belief. In order to understand what he says about this question, it's necessary to know something of the theory of knowledge offered by Alston, and I'll begin with some brief comments on that.

Alston begins by explaining and defending the idea that Christians (and others; but I limit the argument, as does Alston, to Christians) may properly think of themselves as perceiving God in much the same way as they perceive trees or tables. This isn't to say that God is much like a tree or a table. It's rather to say that a conceptual analysis of what it is to perceive a tree and what it is to perceive God yields essentially the same result. So, what it means for John of the Cross or Angela of Foligno (both Christian saints) to perceive God is just that God appears to them in some specifiable way – as loving, as angry, as delivering a message or a commission, and so forth. The claim to which assent is provoked by such broadly perceptual experiences might be *God is loving me now* or *God is speaking to me now*. Given this understanding of what it is to perceive God, Alston's central question is then about the epistemic status of the assents provoked by such experience. Are they warranted or justified – do they have positive epistemic status? Or do they not? If they do have such status, why, and to what degree?

Alston approaches this question by using the notion of a doxastic practice. This is a practice whose outputs or products are beliefs (*doxa* is Greek for opinion, or judgment, or assent). It is, therefore, a belief-forming or belief-producing practice. We engage in many of these, some perceptual (we may form beliefs about how many people are in the room by using our eyes), and some not (we may form beliefs about whether

every even number can be expressed as the sum of two primes by performing some mathematical calculations). Inhabiting a Christian form of
life is one such practice: among its outputs or results are assents of various
sorts, some perceptual (God is on my tongue as I consume the conse-
crated host), and some not (God the Father and God the Son are best
understood as sharing all properties except those of begetting – exclusive
to the Father – and being begotten – exclusive to the Son). Alston limits
his investigation to perceptual beliefs formed by inhabiting a Christian
form of life.

He argues that the question of whether a particular assent has positive
epistemic status can best be answered by asking whether the doxastic practice that produced it is reliable – whether, as he puts it, it "can be
relied on to produce mostly true beliefs."[3] To ask whether Christian
doxastic practice is reliable is then to ask whether "it would yield mostly
true beliefs in a sufficiently large and varied run of employments in
situations of the sorts we typically encounter."[4] Alston explores various
strategies commonly used to show that a doxastic practice is reliable. Many
of them try to demonstrate the reliability of a practice without already
assuming that the practice is reliable. For example, those concerned to
show that ordinary sensory practice (the use of our physical senses to
produce assents about the environment in which we live) is reliable
have often tried to do so without using the assumption that it is reliable
as part of the argument whose conclusion is supposed to be that it is
reliable. But this turns out to be difficult to do; indeed, in Alston's view
it is impossible to do for sensory practice. As he sees it, all arguments
whose conclusion is *sensory practice is reliable* have just this claim among
their assumptions. This is, he thinks, true of most doxastic practices, including Christian practice: attempts to show that it is reliable will, like those
attempting to show that sensory practice is reliable, exhibit the kind of
circularity just mentioned.

This conclusion is controversial. You may reasonably doubt it, as do
many philosophers. If you do, though, the onus will be upon you to offer
an argument whose conclusion is that sensory practice (or Christian practice) is reliable which does not exhibit the circularity that Alston thinks
it inevitably must. That enterprise, though, is not of further interest here.
Suppose we allow Alston the conclusion that noncircular arguments as to
the reliability of a doxastic practice are typically not available. Does it then
follow that it's unreasonable to think of any doxastic practice as reliable?
Not according to Alston. He suggests that when the question of the possible reliability of a doxastic practice in which you engage (Christian prac-

tice if you're a Christian, Buddhist practice if you're a Buddhist) comes up, you should take the position that your practice is reliable, and therefore that its outputs bear positive epistemic status for you – but you should take this position only in a prima facie (at first blush) sense, which is to say that you should acknowledge that your assent to the claim *Christian practice is reliable* might be overridden or defeated. The tactic here is familiar: doxastic practices ought in general to be considered innocent (reliable) until proven guilty (unreliable, or otherwise problematic). But we ought, according to Alston, also to acknowledge that any particular doxastic practice may turn out not to be reliable: that is, that we may come to know of defeaters or overriders to the claim that Christian practice is reliable (or that sensory practice is), and as a result abandon it.

Given all this (and recall that our interest here is not in assessing whether Alston is right or wrong in the substance of the epistemology he offers), it must now be asked whether a Christian's coming to know that there are alien religious doxastic practices – those whose outputs are assents incompatible with those of Christian practice – should call into question the view *Christian practice is reliable*, and as a result reduce (or even remove) epistemic confidence in its particular outputs.

Alston thinks that your knowing of "massive and persistent inconsistency between the outputs of two practices"[5] is reason for you to regard at least one of the practices as unreliable. For example, the outputs of the doxastic practice of consulting horoscopes may be beliefs about the future; but if these are massively and persistently contradicted by ordinary sensory practice when the future becomes present (my 1998 horoscope might say that I will inherit a fortune in 1999, but as midnight strikes at the end of 1999 I find myself without an inherited fortune), then one or another of the doxastic practices is likely to be abandoned or significantly modified. Is it then the case that massive and persistent inconsistency between the outputs of Christian practice and (say) Buddhist practice (should it obtain) ought to lead to abandonment of one or another (or both) – or at least to a significant reduction in epistemic confidence about the outputs of one or another (or both)? This is the Alstonian form of the central question of this chapter.

There's an important difference between the horoscope-vs.-sensory-practice example and the Christian-vs.-Buddhist-practice example. In the first case, the horoscope-caster must, like it or not, also form beliefs by using sensory practice: as the clock strikes midnight on 31 December 1999 the horoscope-user can't help but know (and in part have come to do so sensorily) whether or not she is now rich by inheritance. Some adjustment to confidence in or interpretation of the practices therefore cannot be avoided since the horoscope-user is also necessarily a user of sensory practice. But the user of Christian practice will typically not also be a user of Buddhist practice (and on some understandings of the two practices, cannot be – see the comments in chapter 1 on the impossibility of simultaneously inhabiting two forms of religious life), and so no adjustment in confidence or construal need be immediately required.

But still, some such adjustments may be suggested. The fact that not everyone engages in Christian practice, and that, as a result, not everyone assents to its outputs, is not by itself troubling to Alston. He thinks that there is no reason to suppose that lack of universal distribution of a particular doxastic practice calls its outputs into question. How many people engage in the practice of forming beliefs by the use of mathematical proofs? That the answer is "not many" does nothing, from Alston's viewpoint, to suggest that mathematical practice is doxastically unreliable. Perhaps, then, what really causes epistemic trouble is the fact that explanations of diversity in religious assent can be offered whose entailment is that no religious practice is reliable as a producer of true beliefs. Those who explain diversity in religious assents by characterizing all of them as expressions of private preference offer such an explanation, as do those who see all religious assents as projections of fear or desire. But Alston thinks that this sort of move does not provide a serious epistemic challenge to Christians (or other religious people), either. The fact that there is serious and deep-going disagreement among outputs doesn't mean that an explanation of this fact that removes epistemic confidence in all such outputs is better than one that permits the possibility that some among the incompatible claims generated are true and some false – an explanation, for example, that explains incompatibility by appeal to the difficulty of the subject-matter. Such, presumably, would be the line taken by macro-economists about incompatibilities in the beliefs held by different schools of macro-economists. But there still does remain a difficulty, and Alston puts it like this (what follows is, as he sees it, a summary of the strongest and most defensible argument from religious diversity to the unreliability of any particular religious doxastic practice):

> Each of our rival [religious doxastic] practices is confronted with a plurality of uneliminated alternatives. Thus, in the absence of some sufficient independent reason, no one is justified in supposing her own practice to be superior in epistemic status to those with which it is in competition. And

hence, in this situation no one is being rational in proceeding to employ that practice to form beliefs and to regard beliefs so formed as ipso facto justified.[6]

A "sufficient independent reason" would be a reason independent of engagement in any competing religious doxastic practice, and so also a reason independent of the assumed truth of any of the outputs of such a doxastic practice. Alston thinks that there may in fact be such sufficient independent reasons (and since he is a Christian, he thinks that they would demonstrate the reliability of Christian practice; Christians differ about whether there are such reasons – I, for example, though a Christian, do not think there are); but he admits that it is difficult to say just what they are, and so he concedes for the sake of the argument that there are no such reasons, and proceeds to argue that even this strong argument has only limited epistemic force.

A plurality of uneliminated alternative doxastic practices is not, says Alston, known only in the case of religion. It is evident too (for example) in the practice of diagnosing and treating neurosis: Freudian psychoanalysts will diagnose and treat neurosis differently than will Skinnerian behaviorists. The two doxastic practices will produce incompatible beliefs (and incompatible practices), and there will be no practice-neutral method of determining which (if either) generates true beliefs and efficacious treatments. However, this does not make it irrational to continue engaging in one practice or the other – it does not, that is, greatly reduce the epistemic confidence with which the practitioner of psychoanalysis treats the beliefs that are among the outputs of his practice. As Alston puts it:

> In the absence of any external reason for supposing that one of the competing practices is more accurate than my own, the only rational course for me is to sit tight with the practice of which I am a master and which serves me so well in guiding my activity in the world.[7]

Coming to know of the sheer existence of uneliminated alternatives – at least where there is also no practice-neutral criterion of adjudication – is therefore not seen by Alston as requiring the abandonment of a doxastic practice in which you are already engaged. This is so, anyway, if the doxastic practice in question has a goodly selection from the other marks of reliability discussed at length elsewhere in Alston's work – marks that include *being well-established* and *providing significant self-support*.

Alston concludes that, although knowing about diversity of religious assent should not drastically reduce epistemic confidence (much less require the abandonment of the home religion), it does and should, nonetheless, have some negative epistemic effect for Christians. Christians, he says, typically lose some epistemic confidence when they come to know that different religions generate incompatible assents, which is to say that they'd be more confident did they not know this (and ideally they would not know it because it would not be the case). But the reduction in confidence is not such, he thinks, that it makes continuing to engage in Christian practice irrational once religious diversity is known.

Alston's views on the epistemic significance of awareness of religious diversity usefully illustrate the range of questions that will inevitably require treatment if the issue is seriously to be discussed. First, there are the epistemic questions raised by our coming to know of diversity of assent in any sphere whatever. Dealing with these will in turn require a general epistemological theory. Alston offers such a theory, as we've seen, by developing the idea of reliable doxastic practices; this is certainly not the only option, but it is a specimen of the kind of thing that will have to be done. Then, once some epistemology has been applied to the general question of the epistemic significance of knowledge of diversity, it will have to be applied to the more particular question of the knowledge of diversity in religious assents. And this question will either have to be approached through some general theory of religion, so that an answer can be given that will be usefully applicable to every particular religion, or through analysis of some religion's particulars with the goal of showing what adherents of that religion should think in response to the challenge of epistemic confidence posed by coming to know of religious diversity. Alston's route is, for the most part, this second one: the comments he offers are based upon a particular understanding of Christianity, and their relevance is mostly to inhabitants of that religion.

A full-scale engagement with Alston's views about the epistemic significance of knowledge of religious diversity (or with any views on the matter of comparable scope) would require discussion of all these questions; and that is not within the range of this chapter or this book. I shall suggest only that, even if Alston's general epistemological approach is adopted, there is considerably more to be said than he says about what the Christian account of things suggests on this question. (There would be equally detailed and complex things to say about what the particulars of Buddhist or Islamic accounts of things suggest on the question.) I'll make a few brief suggestions here in terms of the three variables discussed earlier in this chapter, couching them now in Alston's doxastic-practice idiom.

First, are the assents produced by engagement in Christian practice typically accompanied by a high degree of epistemic confidence? Some of them certainly are; Christians have tended to use "faith" as a label for a deep, unshakable confidence in some of the assents suggested or required by inhabiting the Christian form of life. To say, as for example Catholic Christians do (though there are analogous ideas expressed by other Christians) that assent to some claims is *de fide* (a matter of faith) is in part to say that claims so assented to have been revealed by God; this implies that those who assent to them may and should do so with a very high degree of epistemic confidence. What better credentials could a claim have? Not all assents or acceptances made by Christians have claims of this sort as their object, of course; but those that do are unlikely to have the high level of epistemic confidence that accompanies them reduced by one's coming to know (for example) that Muslims make assents whose objects seem to them of the same sort (claims revealed by God), make them with an equally high level of epistemic confidence, and yet make them to (some) claims that cannot be true if (some) Christian claims are true. A rational response by Christians coming to know of this situation is not the abandonment or significant reduction of epistemic confidence in their assents, but rather the judgment that Muslims have gotten things wrong. Likewise, a rational response by Muslims would be the judgment that Christians have gotten things wrong. Most Christians and most Muslims, in the past and now, either have made or would make (were the facts explained) just these judgments. That this is so indicates an important fact about epistemic responses to knowledge of religious diversity, a fact I've already mentioned but which deserves to be underscored again at this point. It's the fact that the degree of epistemic confidence with which an assent is made is typically derived from some conviction about the way the world is (an ontological conviction) – in the case under discussion, the conviction that God has revealed a particular claim to be held *de fide*. It may not be the case that God actually has revealed this claim, of course; but knowing that a religious alien assents to its contradictory *de fide* does not by itself call into question the claim that God has revealed this claim, and it is because of this that Christians are not likely to be (and should not be) epistemically troubled by their coming to know of incompatible assents made *de fide* by religious aliens.

Second, do Christians have reason to think religious aliens trustworthy or authoritative as advocates of claims about God, or human beings, or the environment in which humans live? The answer to this is a qualified affirmative, mostly for the reasons set out in the discussion of open vs. closed inclusivism on the question of truth (in chapter 2). It was suggested there, you may recall, that there are good Christian reasons for thinking that religious aliens can have knowledge of God and are capable of some degree of right response to God. I won't here go over that discussion again; but if the reasons there given are at all convincing, the fact that Christians should so think ought, to some degree, to moderate epistemic confidence when diversity in religious assent comes to be known.

But the extent to which such moderation ought to occur will depend largely upon the ability of those who inhabit the Christian form of life to explain or account for the facts of diversity – most especially the fact that some religious aliens assent to incompatible claims *de fide*. And here matters become a little more complicated – or at least, the range of opinion which is defensible as Christian is broader. At one end of the spectrum are those who think that all alien religions ought be understood by Christians as inhabited by those sunk in sin, oppressed by the weight of depravity inherited from Adam – who think, in other words, that it is entirely to be expected that there be alien assent *de fide* to some claims about God and humans that must be false if Christian claims are true. Surprise, on this view, is the correct response not when this situation obtains (for given the reality of sin, of course it does), but rather when there is agreement between alien teaching and Christian teaching. This view is easily capable of explaining deep diversity in religious assents (its adherents will probably also advocate closed inclusivism on truth), and those who hold it are unlikely to be epistemically troubled by coming to know of deep diversity. But at the other end of the spectrum are more optimistic views about the cognitive capacities of religious aliens. On these views, deep diversity is harder to predict and explain because God is not understood to have restricted his illuminating presence to those who explicitly know of Jesus and the Holy Spirit. Holders of such views will be and should be more troubled than those at the other end of the spectrum by knowledge of deep diversity, and this is principally because they do not expect it and find it difficult to explain.

Decisions on the matters just mentioned will require work in theology as well as philosophy, and such work can neither be carried out nor properly represented here. I shall simply register, without further argument, the opinion that Christians ought to be moderately epistemically troubled by knowledge of deep religious diversity because this is not something easily predictable from properly Christian theological assumptions (which is not to say that what might be called shallow diversity is surprising or unpredictable on Christian assumptions), and because it does (and should) raise questions about whether error can enter the Christian account of things – and, if it can, how it does so, how deep it may go, and how it ought to be recognized and controlled. I don't mean by this that knowledge of deep diversity should significantly reduce epistemic confidence in Christian doctrine, much less that it should issue in abandonment of assent to it. But I do mean that the epistemic uneasiness often (and properly) produced by increasing Christian awareness of deep diversity should be acknowledged as a neuralgic point of creative conceptual growth for Christian thought, of the same order of importance, perhaps, as is attention to the question of apparently unmerited suffering.

This brief sketch of a Christian response to the question of epistemic confidence could and should be paralleled by those working from within the conceptual constraints of other traditions. Any such sketch will (as the one I've offered does) illustrate the general truth that serious thought by the religiously committed about the epistemic questions raised by knowledge of deep diversity will have to be done in constant awareness of the particular commitments of that religion. The epistemic obligations of religious people, in this or any other matter, cannot be assessed independently of judgments about the truth of these commitments. For the nonreligious, as we've seen, matters are different; they will likely feel pulled, by their coming to know of deep diversity of assent in religious matters, toward the conclusion that all such assents are on an epistemic par, and this move will in turn almost inevitably result in the conclusion that religious assents are a matter of private preference. But in the case of the religious, as of the nonreligious, consideration of the epistemic questions raised by knowledge of religious diversity involves (is properly an aspect of) considering how to treat the religious alien. And this is the central topic of chapter 4, to which I now turn.

## NOTES

1   *United States Reports*, vol. 505 (Washington, D.C.: US Government Printing Office, 1996), p. 851.

2   William James, *The Varieties of Religious Experience*, in James, *Writings: 1902–1910* (New York: Literary Classics of the United States, 1987), pp. 1–477, at p. 36.

3   William P. Alston, *Perceiving God: The Epistemology of Religious Experience* (Ithaca & London: Cornell University Press, 1991), p. 101.
4   Ibid., pp. 104–5.
5   Ibid., 171.
6   Ibid., p. 270.
7   Ibid., p. 274.

# CHAPTER 4

# The Religious Alien

What attitudes toward the religious alien are possible? This is the central question of this chapter. Closely associated questions are: How may religious aliens be treated? What patterns of behavior toward them might be recommended? The questions of chapters 2 (about truth) and 3 (about epistemic confidence) might be understood as elements within this broader question. But my interest in this chapter is not in religious assents in the light of religious diversity, as it was in both of those; my interest here is in a complex of questions that center upon religious aliens as such rather than upon what they believe or do.

This is a question for both the religious and the nonreligious, since for both contact with religious aliens is almost unavoidable, as is some decision about their proper treatment. It is conceivable that someone (religious or nonreligious) could avoid this question by finding himself in a situation in which no religious aliens are present. A society in which everyone is Buddhist or everyone Muslim might be such; so might one in which no one is religious. Perhaps there were more such situations in the past than there are now – situations in which a life might be spent without meeting or having to think about religious aliens. While such situations are not utterly absent now (perhaps you might spend a life in a small Minnesota town meeting only Lutheran Christians; or one in a small Sri Lankan village meeting only Buddhists; or one in an English university meeting only the nonreligious), they are no longer common; and even where they are approached, the news media will likely bring the religious alien into your presence whether you like it or not.

In virtually every contemporary democratic state, certainly, consideration of how the religious alien should be treated is part of what gets talked about in the public square. There will usually be constitutional provisions that speak to it (the United States and India provide perhaps the most interesting cases of this); there will almost always be legislation or judicial action directly addressed to it (the English courts have had to decide such matters as whether turban-wearing Sikhs may be exempted from laws requiring helmets for motorcycle riders); and there are almost always vocal religious groups whose forms of life require them, as they see it, to speak to matters of concern to the whole of the body politic, and to do so loudly enough that most citizens cannot avoid hearing them. No citizen of such a state (and this now means most people), therefore, can completely avoid consideration of the questions to be treated in this chapter.

This question is different from the questions of chapters 2 and 3 in another way. Those questions, about truth and epistemic confidence, can be discussed independently of religious diversity, even though particular versions of them are raised by religious diversity. But the questions of this chapter are raised only by religious diversity; it makes no sense to consider how the religious alien should be treated if there are no religious aliens.

In spite of these differences, answers that might be given to the question of how the religious alien ought to be treated are likely to be interwoven with answers given to the questions of truth and epistemic confidence. What you think about the possible truth of religious claims and the degree of epistemic confidence that should be given to religious assents will (or at least ought to) be linked with what you think about the proper treatment of the religious alien. But these connections will be neither straightforward nor simple. You might, for example, think that toleration is the key attitude to be encouraged toward the religious alien largely because you think that all religious claims are on a par with respect to truth; or, you might think the same thing about toleration because you think that all alien religious claims are false but that toleration is required by the particulars of your religious account of things. Or, you might think that the ideal way to respond to religious aliens is to attempt to convince them that they should no longer inhabit their particular religious form of life. And you might think this either because you judge it better for them to abandon a dangerously misleading religious account of things and to replace it with a better one; or, equally likely, because you think that all religious forms of life are dangerously misleading, and you'd rather that all religious people should become nonreligious.

The main responses to the question of how the religious alien should be treated are: with toleration; by separation; and as an object of conversion. Combinations of these are possible, too, as we shall see. But these three expressions label relatively distinct types of response, and I'll consider them in order.

## 4.1   Toleration: Enduring the Religious Alien

To tolerate something (some action or behavior or event) is to permit it to be what it is without interference or coercion. Toleration in this sense (there are others) carries with it also the connotation of dislike or neutrality: you tolerate, or put up with, actions or events that you would prefer not to be occurring, or in whose occurrence you have no interest; you don't tolerate something you like or are happy about – or at least it sounds odd to say that you do. I tolerate my allergies (I put up with them without trying to alter or destroy them) not because I like them but because my experience has been that attempting to interfere with them or remove them by medication is worse for me than is letting them run their course. But although I treat my friends like my allergies in the sense that I do not (on the whole) interfere with them or attempt to coerce them into being other than they are, it sounds odd to say that I tolerate them. And this is because my friends, unlike my allergies, are a pleasure and a benefit to me; I don't have to tolerate them precisely because I like them. John Courtney Murray puts the point elegantly:

> Tolerance is a concept of the moral order. It implies a moral judgment on error and the consequent adoption of a moral attitude, based on charity, toward the good faith of those who err.[1]

Toleration, therefore, marks a refusal to interfere with something you don't like or are neutral towards, an affirmation that whatever is the object of your toleration ought to be let be. Toleration's absence is discernible to the extent that interference or coercion is evident. Those who advocate toleration and attempt to practice it will, if they are consistent, do nothing directly to interfere with what they are trying to tolerate. They will certainly not attempt to destroy or significantly alter the objects of their toleration, and they may often speak and think of their policy of noninterference in terms of the rights of those whom they tolerate to think and act as they do. This kind of toleration is usefully thought of as negative: it does nothing to interfere, but it also does nothing to support. I might be tolerant of your advocacy of anti-Semitism in this sense. If I am, I won't interfere with your advocacy, and may, if pressed, say that no one else ought to, either. But if I'm only negatively tolerant of your anti-Semitism, I won't do anything to preserve and protect it if it comes under threat. If I do so act – perhaps I'm a member of the American Civil Liberties Union, and will donate money and time to support your right to distribute materials advocating anti-Semitism – then I'm not only negatively tolerant but also positively tolerant. Positive toleration, then, adds to a negatively tolerant judgment (that what's being tolerated should be let be) a positively tolerant judgment (that what's being tolerated should be actively protected or supported – certainly when threatened, but perhaps also more generally).

These are clearly attitudes that can be had and encouraged toward the religious alien. They are also attitudes that may be commended as much by the religiously committed as by the nonreligious (though typically for different reasons). And, finally, they are attitudes much commended in the public discourse of late-capitalist democracies at the beginning of the twenty-first century. To say in such a context that someone is intolerant is to insult her, just as to say of someone that she's tolerant is to praise her. This broad cultural commendation of toleration is evident also in political and judicial rhetoric: it's often said that toleration (especially religious toleration) is characteristic of democracy, and that this is one of the good things about democracy.

But there are interesting philosophical questions to be raised about toleration of the religious alien. The first is that of scope: How far can toleration of the religious alien extend? Some speak and write as though it can and ought to be universal, as though all religious aliens, together with everything advocated, done, and believed by them ought to be and can be tolerated. Others appear to think that the scope of toleration must be more limited than this, that there is some selection of religiously alien practices and beliefs (and perhaps some selection of religious aliens) that require tolerance, while others are beyond its scope. There is also the question of the agent: who is it that ought to be tolerant? For some it may be the individual; for others the state or the church or some other corporate body; and for yet others, both. It does seem possible to think (though the details will be complicated) that, for instance, the state ought to be tolerant of religious aliens, though individuals need not be (or, with still more difficulty, the other way around). These questions could be pursued at length in an abstract way; but it will likely be more productive to have an interlocutor before us, and so I'll now offer some comments on toleration as it was treated by the English philosopher John

Locke (1632–1704). His thought shows, with elegant clarity, the strengths and the limits of the idea of toleration.

Locke wrote extensively on political theory in a social context marked by deep religious division. England after the Civil War (1642–8) was politically torn by divisions between Catholics (Locke prefers "papists") and radical Protestants (Locke prefers "dissenters," or, sometimes, "fanatics"), and Locke's writings had a good deal of influence upon attempts to resolve the situation. In a number of his works he addresses the question of religious toleration explicitly, most clearly and usefully in the *Essay Concerning Toleration* (1667), and the *Letter On Toleration* (1685), upon both of which I'll draw in the comments that follow.[2] Locke's remarks in these works were important not only for the English context, but also for their formative influence upon the patterns of thought that underlie the American constitutional position on religion. Understanding what he thought about the matter, then, will help not only with the logic of the idea of toleration, but also with the contemporary situation in the United States. Locke is interesting on this issue, too, because he offers arguments for the state's toleration of religion both from a religiously-uncommitted standpoint, and from a Christian (though dubiously orthodox) position. His main concern is with toleration of the religious alien as an attitude proper to the state (which he usually calls "the commonwealth" and personifies as "the magistrate," who is both maker and enforcer of law), rather than as an attitude to be commended for the individual (though he does commend it there, too).

Locke's position depends upon a sharp distinction between the domain of the state and that of the church — which is the same as that of religion. These two domains must be capable of strict theoretical separation in order for Locke's advocacy of toleration to be tenable, and he defines them in such a way that they are.

"The commonwealth," he says, "seems to me to be a society of men constituted only for the procuring, preserving, and advancing of their own civil interests."[3] These interests include, and are paradigmatically represented by, life, liberty, health, and private property. The duty of the magistrate, operating within this domain, is to do just and only what preserves and nurtures these goods; nothing more and nothing less. Anything that has no direct relation to these goods can have no effect upon the magistrate's purposes, and therefore falls entirely outside his domain. His only duty with respect to such things is to tolerate them. They have an "absolute and universal right to toleration,"[4] which is to say that the magistrate should do nothing to them other than leave them alone.

A church, by contrast, is "a voluntary society of men, joining themselves together of their own accord in order to the public worshipping of God, in such a manner as they judge acceptable to him, and effectual to the salvation of their souls."[5] The business of churches, on Locke's understanding, is the salvation of souls, and more particularly the patterns of worship that seem to those who choose to join them (note the term "voluntary") best designed to bring about that goal. Just as the state can have nothing directly to say to this business, so the church can have nothing directly to say to the state's business of assuring life, liberty, property, and so forth. The two domains do not, in their ideal-typical forms, overlap in the least.

This lack of overlap provides the first element in Locke's argument for religious toleration on the part of the magistrate. Since what churches do is out of the magistrate's domain, he is incapable of discerning correctness in religious opinion and equally incapable of legislating it. The magistrate has equally little to do with the care of souls, with the proper mode of worship, or with anything else that churches are interested in. The following passage is entirely representative in its emphasis upon the sheer irrelevance of the particulars of religious observance to the interests of the state:

> For kneeling or sitting in the sacrament can in itself tend no more to the disturbance of the government or injury of my neighbour than sitting or standing at my own table; wearing a cope or surplice in the church can no more in its own nature alarm or threaten the peace of the state than wearing a cloak or coat in the market; being rebaptized no more make a tempest in the commonwealth than it doth in the river, nor than barely washing myself would do in either. If I observe the Friday with the Mahometan, or the Saturday with the Jew, or the Sunday with the Christian . . . I see nothing in any of these, if they be done sincerely and out of conscience, that can of itself make me either the worse subject to my prince, or worse neighbour to my fellow-subject.[6]

It is just because of this radical separation, just because what you do as a religious person makes you neither better nor worse as a citizen, that the magistrate ought to leave the religious alien alone. Further, for the magistrate (Americans might say, for the legislature, judiciary, and executive together), everyone is a religious alien, since it follows from the definitions given by Locke of the interests of the state and those of the churches that it would be nonsensical to say that the state could itself have a religious identity. As he often says, there can on his understanding be no such thing as a Christian commonwealth, since nothing about Christianity requires or suggests the establishment of one, of a body politic governed by civil laws. These things are simply not the business of Christianity, from which it follows that although any magistrate may be a Christian, he is not acting as a Christian when he acts as a magistrate. It's interesting to notice that Locke does allow the possibility of a Jewish commonwealth because in it the magistrate is, in a certain sense, Yahweh, the law-giving God. But to the extent that this is so, Judaism is not properly a church on Locke's understanding, but rather combines characteristics of both church and commonwealth.[7]

The state, then, when acting as such in the person of the magistrate, ought to tolerate religion in the sense of leaving it alone. But this is not all. Locke also thinks that (Christian) churches have Christian reasons for tolerating the religious alien: "I esteem that toleration to be the chief characteristical mark of the true Church."[8] What are these specifically Christian reasons? Chief among them is charity, the love advocated by the New Testament. For Christians, says Locke, love is the chief instrument of faith, and this means that anything opposed to what Christians understand the Gospel to be, whether the vices of Christians or the errors of religious aliens, ought never to be opposed by force and compulsion. Christians neither do nor ought attempt to coerce good morals among Christians; similarly, they should not attempt to coerce right worship or correct religious assent among religious aliens.[9] Any offenses against toleration of this sort are, by definition, not Christian. The conclusion is:

> Nobody therefore, in fine, neither single persons, nor Churches, nay, nor even commonwealths, have any just title to invade the civil rights and worldly goods of each other, upon pretence of religion.[10]

The duty to religious toleration is universal because the state and the church have been defined in such a way that each is irrelevant to the other.

But there are difficulties. Chief among them is the unfortunate fact that religious people, members of churches, have opinions and advocate practices that seem to them required by their religion (indeed, intrinsic to their religion), and that do impinge, negatively, upon the goals and purposes of the state. Paradigmatic among these, for Locke, is the papist claim that loyalty is to be given to the Pope over every other prince.[11] But there are also habits of association that seem to those who engage in them to be religious, habits that bring people into a "stricter confederacy with those of their own denomination and party than other their fellow subjects."[12] Locke has in mind here both Catholics and dissenting (non-Anglican) Protestants. In general, if any of these groups forms habits or attitudes of loyalty to anything (other Quakers, other Lutherans) or anyone (the Pope) that calls into question or dilutes their loyalty to the magistrate on matters of concern to the commonwealth – and these matters of concern are, recall, principally the preservation of life, liberty, and private property – then what was religion has ceased to be properly so and has become a potential or actual danger to the state. Locke acknowledges that this situation is common, and that when it arises it marks the limits of toleration on the part of the magistrate, though it still permits the claim that religious toleration should be universal, since the states of affairs that require the intervention of the magistrate are no longer (according to Locke's definition) properly religious.

When the magistrate perceives such situations, he "may and ought to use all ways either of policy or power, that shall be convenient to lessen, break, and suppress the [religious] party, and so prevent the mischief."[13] Locke urges the magistrate to avoid the use of force whenever possible in such cases, but acknowledges that sometimes it will be necessary to use it. This doesn't sound much like religious toleration. It sounds even less like it when we remind ourselves that Locke considered it perfectly proper for the English commonwealth to restrict Catholic publishing, and to punish Catholics just for being such – even to the point of executing them.[14] Locke also says, dramatically: "[T]hose are not at all to be tolerated who deny the being of a God."[15] This sounds like a charter for the state to coerce the nonreligious into being so. Locke's reason for saying this is that nontheists will typically, he thinks, not be bound by promise, covenant, or oath, and since these bonds are essential to the very existence of human society their absence is intrinsically destructive to the interests and needs of the commonwealth. To be more consistent with his premises, Locke should have said that the magistrate should reserve his intolerance for oath-breaking and the like (matters of action), and not exercise it upon atheism (a matter of belief), even if the latter does lead to the former. That he does not do this suggests an insufficiently sharp distinction between belief and action.

But Locke would say that these actions on the part of the state aren't religious intolerance; they are, rather, the state controlling what it must control if it is to remain a commonwealth, and in so doing, coercing not religion properly understood, but rather religion as misunderstood by some of those who call themselves religious. Religion as such neither can nor should be coerced or constrained by the state; but the side effects or epiphenomena of religion misconstrued sometimes may have to be.

The fundamental principles of Lockean religious toleration are clearly summarized thus:

> Whatsoever is lawful in the commonwealth cannot be prohibited by the magistrate in the Church. Whatsoever is permitted unto any of his subjects for their ordinary use, neither can nor ought to be forbidden by him to any sect of people for their religious uses . . . But those things that are prejudicial to the commonweal of a people in their ordinary use, and are therefore forbidden by laws, those things ought not to be permitted to Churches in their sacred rites.[16]

On this view, if religion remains what it ought to be, it will be tolerated by the state. If, however, it offends against any of the state's proper interests, it will be coerced, just as would any other offender. The principle is that the magistrate's laws are to be applied indifferently, and that where they conflict with what religious people take their reliigon to demand of them, the magistrate's laws must always take precedence. Locke also acknowledges that the magistrate may, like religious people, misunderstand the extent of his own interests and attempt, improperly, to legislate and coerce properly religious matters. When this happens, the offense is as great (and of the same logical kind) as when religious people misunderstand their religion as requiring them to encroach upon and offend against the interests of the commonwealth.

Locke's views about the importance of toleration as an attitude to the religious alien apply most directly to the nonreligious state. They require toleration (noninterference, absence of coercion, letting be) of all properly religious behavior on the part of the nonreligious state. The First Amendment to the Constitution of the United States is a direct descendant of Locke on this matter, for its religion clauses also imply that the state should not itself be religious, and they directly state that it should not coerce (positively or negatively) religious belief or behavior on the part of its citizens. The Lockean position and the United States Constitutional position are similar, too, in that they both commend religious toleration to the state by separating the domain in which the state holds sway from that in which religion holds sway. This is entirely typical of proposals for religious toleration by a nonreligious state. In order for such proposals to work, it must be the case that what religious aliens do and propose is located in a domain separate from (and ideally irrelevant to) that of the state's interests – most commonly, perhaps, in a private domain. For if the various religious forms of life are not so located, if some or all of what they recommend is directly relevant to (a proper part of) what the state is interested in, then the state will have to legislate and coerce on religious matters, and in so doing will have to abandon toleration.

And it is beyond doubt that, on the understanding of religion in play in this book, much of what is taken by inhabitants of particular religious forms of life to be required of them as such is in fact directly relevant to and does in fact directly impinge upon the interests of the Lockean state, as it also does upon the interests of the European and American democracies at the turn of the millennium. Many Christians and Jews, for example, find it impossible to reconcile the legality of abortion in most of those democracies with what is required of them by their identity as Christians and Jews. Many Muslims, perhaps, would wish that the provisions of American civil and criminal law coincided with those of the Qur'an and the Hadith and, to the extent that they do not, find them unacceptable. Indeed, since the understanding of religion in play here sees being religious as inhabiting a form of life that seems comprehensive and unsurpassable to those who inhabit it, the idea that it could seem to religious people that there is a sphere (that of the state's interests) separate from and irrelevant to their Christian (or Jewish or Buddhist) identity is an extremely odd one. Instead, it will be quite typical that religious people will understand their religious identity to have direct implications for what the state should do. And if this fact is coupled with the fact that different religious forms of life propose different and noncompossible modes of action for the state (make abortion illegal/don't make abortion illegal; permit racial intermarriage/don't permit racial intermarriage; provide a tax policy that favors heterosexual marriage over being single/don't provide a tax policy that favors heterosexual marriage over being single – and so on), it follows directly that the state cannot maintain a stance of toleration towards all religious behaviors. Some it will have to make legal; others it will have to make illegal. Some it will have to support; others it will have to persecute. A similar problem arises here as was evident in the attempt to see all religious claims as on a par with respect to truth (discussed in chapter 2).

Locke, as we've seen, recognizes this with beautiful clarity, and as a result does not shrink from recommending the persecution of Catholics and atheists by the state. He makes the definitional move of saying that what the state persecutes in these cases is not religious claims or behavior, properly understood, but rather claims and behavior epiphenomenal to religion. And he must make this move because he has defined the domains of religion and of the state as not impinging one upon the other. Persecution of Catholics is therefore understood by him not as religious persecution but rather as a proper defense by the state of state interests.

Similar moves are evident in the history of interpretation of the United States Constitution, though not usually stated with Lockean clarity. The Constitution has been read to comport well with the use of military force by the United States to enforce monogamous marriage upon members of the Church of Jesus Christ of Latter Day Saints (Mormons). And, more recently, it has been read to comport well with the punishment of Native Americans for using peyote in religious ritual. Decisions on matters of this kind always come down to the question of whether the state's legitimate interests (in supporting monogamous heterosexual marriage or in preventing the use of hallucinogenic drugs in the two instances mentioned) ought to outweigh the state's presumption in favor of religious toleration. Often, they are seen to; and on at least some occasions, it is implicit in such decisions that the behavior being constrained or coerced by the state ought not to be regarded as genuinely religious. This definitional separation of what is properly religious from the domain of what it is in the interest of a democratic polity to control is almost always evident in philosophical analyses of religious freedom.

This is not to say, however, that either the religion clauses of the First Amendment or the tradition of their interpretation by the courts are in every respect Lockean. Where they are most dramatically not so is in their refusal of the Lockean presumption that the laws of the commonwealth ought to be applied indifferently to the religious and the nonreligious. The United States Constitution (as interpreted by the courts) does not take this view. There is a long history of exceptions to and exemptions from constraint by state or federal laws for the religious: Quakers and Mennonites have been exempted from military conscription because of their pacifist beliefs; the Amish have been exempted from the requirement of full-time school attendance beyond the eighth grade; and, of course, anything recognized as a church by the Internal Revenue Service is exempted from tax requirements incumbent upon all other corporate bodies.

But these distinctions do not make a difference so far as concerns the central conceptual features of the recommendation to the nonreligious of toleration as the proper attitude toward the religious alien. On the understanding of religion in play in this book such a recommendation cannot consistently be acted upon, whether by a nonreligious state or a nonreligious individual; and it is just because it cannot consistently be acted upon that there are no instances of its being consistently acted upon. Where the rhetoric of toleration's desirability is found, the reality will always be that some religious proposals are tolerated and others are not. And where the state is supposed to be religiously tolerant, the reality will always be that some religious proposals are constrained and coerced by force while others are not. Sometimes the appearance of consistent toleration of the religious alien will be maintained by defining religion in such a way that only those proposals that are tolerable by the state count as religious, or in such a way that there are no noncompossible religious proposals. But this is like making the state consistently nonviolent by the simple expedient of defining violence as that which the state does not do: an Orwellian move rather than a conceptually interesting one.

Toleration of the religiously alien is not, however, recommended only by and to the nonreligious. It is also sometimes recommended (usually in limited terms) from within the confines of particular religious forms of life, and in their terms. Consider the following words of Tenzin Gyatso, the fourteenth Dalai Lama, spoken in a 1982 interview (he is responding to a question about whether he would encourage nonBuddhists to become Buddhist):

> That's a tricky question. Of course, from the Buddhist viewpoint, we are all human beings and we all have every right to investigate either one's own religion or another religion. This is our right. I think that on the whole a comparative study of different religious traditions is useful. I generally believe that every major religion has the potential for giving any human being good advice; there is no question that this is so. But we must always keep in mind that different individuals have different mental predispositions. This means that for some individuals one religious system or philosophy will be more suitable than another. The only way one can come to a proper conclusion as to what is most suitable for oneself is through comparative study. Hence, we look and study, and we find a teaching that is most suitable to our own taste . . . I cannot advise everyone to practice Buddhism. That I cannot do. Certainly, for some people the Buddhist religion or ideology is most suitable, most effective. But that does not mean it is most suitable for all.[17]

This is best understood as a recommendation by one Buddhist to others that Buddhism (at least of the variety espoused by the Dalai Lama) does not require, and may suggest the desirability of renouncing, any efforts to make religious aliens into religious kin. The desire for conversion appears here to be ruled out as a properly Buddhist attitude to the religious alien. This is a recommendation of toleration in the limited sense that it rules out certain sorts of interference with the religious alien; but it can be consistently maintained because it does not require (as does the toleration exercised by the Lockean magistrate) the establishment of a religion-neutral space, or of a theory about which aspects of human behavior can be isolated from (or held to relate identically to) the requirements of any and all religions. Instead, it derives a particular recommendation for the inhabitants of the home religion directly from the doctrinal commitments of that religion.

There are other possibilities in this line. A particular religion might require its inhabitants to isolate themselves from all religious aliens, to have nothing to do with them or their teachings. This too (though with a little more difficulty, as I'll suggest when I come to discuss the separatist attitude below) can be consistently maintained at the theoretical level, because it also does not require the kind of theoretical commitments about the nature of religion that the Lockean recommendation needs; all it requires is a particular understanding of the needs of the home community and of the implications of its doctrine.

In sum: toleration of all religious proposals from a position of religious neutrality is impossible, unless religion is defined in such a way as to eviscerate it and thereby to make it effectively unrecognizable to faithful Jews, Buddhists, Muslims, Christians, and most others who inhabit forms of life that seem to them comprehensive, unsurpassable, and of central importance. Recommendations of toleration in this sense are therefore incoherent, short of the required definitional sleight of hand. Religion-specific recommendations of particular versions of toleration, however, do not suffer from this difficulty, which provides another example of the interesting phenomenon that reasoning about religious diversity is better done from within the bounds of some particular religious commitment than from without. Naturally, whether toleration is desirable for the inhabitants of any particular religion will depend upon the doctrinal commitments of that religion.

## 4.2 Separation: Isolating the Religious Alien

Separation is a more radical form of toleration. To be tolerant is to decide not to interfere with or coerce those at whom toleration is directed; it is to decide to let them be, which need not require separation from them.

Separation is stronger: it is letting-be by removal. To be separatist is to decide, in the extreme case, to want nothing at all to do with those from whom separation is desired, to decide that all forms of relationship to or connection with them are improper or undesirable. This is the desire for total separation. In a more limited (and more common) case, partial separation may be sought, which is to say separation in only some respects. There is, too, a difference between comprehensive separatism, which is the desire for separation (total or partial) from all others; and noncomprehensive separatism, which is the desire for separation (again, total or partial) from only some others.

The separatist attitude, in all its forms, carries with it various forms of action. Separatists may remove, if they can, those from whom they want separation from their presence, perhaps by exiling them to far-away places, as the ancient Romans used to do to those who were no longer tolerable to the state but did not warrant death, or as the English used to do by transporting criminals to Australia. Or, separatists may keep those from whom they want separation close at hand but ghettoize them by placing them in prisons, or by designating certain areas in which they may live but to which those who create the ghettos or build the prisons need never go. Or, separatists may remove themselves from those from whom they want separation, perhaps by going to a place where they are not, as did many separatist emigrants from Europe to the Americas in the seventeenth and eighteenth centuries, or as some survivalist groups now do in the remote areas of the United States. Or, separatists may do nothing so geographically dramatic, but may simply ensure that their patterns of movement and thought do not bring them into contact with those from whom they want separation. In Chicago, for instance, many residents of the expensive northern suburbs will never go to the south side of the city, and they will avoid this in large part to ensure their continuing separation from the poor (and from their point of view dangerous) people who live there.

Separatist desires may be mutual, which is to say that separatists may be as eager for separation from us as we are for separation from them. Boys and girls in second- and third-grade classrooms are likely to be separatist by mutual consent in this way: without intervention from adult authority they will arrange their seating in the classroom so that no girl has to sit next to a boy. Separation by mutual consent is common, too, in the deeply ethnically and racially segregated patterns of living and worshipping evident in many large American cities (certainly in Chicago, where I live). But separatist desires may also be one-sided, acted on (even compelled) by only one of the parties. Christians compelled Jewish separateness by the establishment of ghettos in some of the cities of Europe in the twelfth century. Men compelled women to be separated from them as students in the ancient universities of England (at least until the twentieth century). And adults compel children to be separated from them when adult dinner-parties take place.

Desire for total separation (separation in all respects, the cutting-off of all forms of relation), even when it is noncomprehensive (directed toward only some others) is difficult to achieve. Attempting it will often involve geographical removal, and will typically require constant vigilance, especially if complete geographical removal turns out not to be possible. If, for instance, a group of men wants total separation from women, the best way to achieve this will be by removing themselves from the possibility of contact with any woman (perhaps by entering a monastery or by becoming hermits). If this can't be managed, extreme vigilance will be necessary, and will probably fail. And, of course, desires for comprehensive separation that is also total will be still more difficult to realize. If, for example, you're Korean, and you want separation of this sort from all non-Koreans, this will mean that you want no relations or connections of any sort with non-Koreans, and this will tend to make life a little complex, even in Korea. The fact that total separation will usually not be achievable does not, however, lessen its interest as a goal. Even when total separation fails to be realized, the desire for it will not typically thereby vanish or be abandoned: those forced by circumstance or pressure into relations with groups from whose members they'd rather be entirely separate will usually still minimize these relations, and in doing so will show themselves still to be total separatists by desire.

The desire for partial separation of a noncomprehensive sort (separation from some others in only some respects) is both more common and more achievable. For example, one group may want to separate itself from another completely in matters of eating and drinking and marriage: the first group won't, perhaps, share food with the second; and no member of the first group will marry any member of the second. But members of the first group may employ members of the second, may be happy to be in close physical proximity to them, to shake hands with them, to talk with them, to exchange money for services with them, to give gifts to their children, and so on. This pattern of relations, characteristic of many forms of class-based separatism, neither intends nor achieves comprehensive separation; but it is separatist with respect to some of the most important aspects of human life.

The desire for comprehensive but partial separation (for separation from all others but not in all respects) is also relatively common and quite easy to achieve. Indeed, in its very partial forms, it is probably unavoidable. Married people are likely to desire separation from all others with respect to sexual relations; Christians are likely to desire separation from all non-Christians with respect to partaking of the eucharist together – and so on.

This relatively formal analysis of the kinds of separatism needs to be supplemented only by some brief comments on motive. Why would individuals or groups be separatist in any of the senses mentioned? In the case of the more moderate kinds of separatism – those, especially, that advocate only partial separation and with respect to fairly few types of relation or connection – no special motive need be looked for. Everyone, without exception, seems to themselves to belong to certain forms of life that have boundaries (recall the discussion in chapter 1 – we are members of a family, worshippers in a church, citizens of a nation, followers of a baseball team, and so on). This requires some separatist desires of us, desires to share some forms of relation only with some and not with all – desires, that is to say, for various kinds of partial separation. It is, however, useful to look for special motives when desires for total separation are found. These are desires for no relations of any kind with at least some alien groups (in the case of total noncomprehensive separatism), or for no relations of any kind with all alien groups (in the case of total comprehensive separatism), and they are much less common than desires for partial separation.

The usual motives for total separatism are fear, and its close correlate, hatred. The judgment that the alien is irrelevant or uninteresting will usually not suffice to produce total separatism; it's more likely, in fact, to issue in the advocacy of toleration. You'll recall that Locke's advocacy of tolerance was based in large part on the view that the enterprises of the commonwealth and those of the church are irrelevant to one another. But separatism replaces the judgment that the alien is irrelevant with the judgment that the alien is in some important respect dangerous, and that as a result continued association with the alien will be damaging to those belonging to the home community. This fear will often go with hatred: whatever you think of as a threat you are likely also to hate. This is why separatist desires are so often accompanied by violence. If the desire for separation is not mutual then separation may need to be brought about and enforced by violence; and even if it is mutual, violence may still be present as a side-effect of the fear each side has of the other. In extreme cases of separatism, this nexus of hatred, fear, and violence is very obvious. Hitler's final solution was the logical culmination of deep Nazi desires for separation from the Jews; it is an ideal-typical case of separatist passions held by a group with power to act on them. Equally deep separatist desires on the part of the powerless are, obviously, much less likely to provoke violence, even when they are as deeply implicated with fear and hatred.

But here a qualification is necessary. Although fear and hatred are likely to be the dominant motives underlying separatism, there will be cases in which they are significantly modified by other motives and attitudes. Imagine a relatively powerless group, surrounded by others, aliens, whose values and modes of life it judges to be irredeemably opposed to its own, as well as intrinsically evil and destructive. Imagine further that the members of this group have no hatred for the aliens, and that even their fear is moderated by an assurance (God-given, perhaps, as they see it) that the aliens will eventually destroy themselves and can pose no threat to themselves because their future is assured – perhaps, again, by God. This group may still be separatist: it may decide that there is no profit to be had from further association with the aliens, and take all the steps it can to see that total separation is approached as closely as may be. But this group may be motivated more by a kind of exhaustion, perhaps mixed with despair, than by fear and hatred. It is even conceivable that there could be deeply separatist groups motivated in their separatism chiefly by a joyful sense of their own special calling, and only minimally by fear, hatred, or suspicion of the alien.

So much, then, for the possible kinds of separatism and for the motives likely to accompany it. How is all this likely to work for religiously committed people? Under what conditions are they likely to be (or become) separatist, and what is to be said, philosophically, about the recommendation of separatist attitudes directed toward the religiously alien? An example will be useful here.

The Old Order Amish Mennonite Church ("Amish" for short – though, strictly, not all "Amish" are members of the Old Order Amish Mennonite Church; schisms and separations in the second half of the nineteenth century have complicated matters, but the generalization will do for my purposes) is a small Protestant Christian denomination (some might prefer to call it a sect) whose members are now to be found mostly in the American Midwest, from Pennsylvania to Iowa. It is descended from a schismatic movement among Swiss Anabaptists at the end of the seventeenth century, and was gradually transplanted to the United States from the beginning of the eighteenth century onwards. It exists now only in the United States (and to a very small extent in Canada), and may include about 50,000 people. It was a strongly separatist movement in its origins, and it has retained that character up to the present day. Amish men and women organize all the major aspects of their social life (dress, work, marriage, education) in ways that mark them as deeply different from those who inhabit the dominant culture that surrounds them. In dress, the men wear broad-brimmed black hats and black homespun suits; the women bonnets and long dresses. Neither wear jewelry or ornamentation of any kind. Many aspects of modern technology, including electricity, the internal combustion engine, and the telephone, are not used at all. Children are usually not given formal education beyond the eighth grade. The community aims at material self-sufficiency, and so it minimizes business and trade contacts with non-Amish: men are not permitted to take a business partner who is not Amish, and the preferred mode of making a living is by farming. Emotional and reproductive self-sufficiency is also an aim, and so marriage with non-Amish is forbidden for both men and women, as are all intimate contacts with outsiders, with "the English" as the Pennsylvania Amish tend to call them. Finally, independence from the political structures of the surrounding culture is also an aim, and so Amish men and women are not permitted to seek or hold elected office or office as a civil servant of any kind; and for the most part they do not vote.

Amish separatism in its ideal-typical form is an attempt at total and comprehensive separation. It applies not only to the religiously alien, but to all who are not Amish. It is, of course, theologically grounded and justified. The Amish tend to think of themselves as a called and chosen people, set apart to serve God in ways that others may not be called to imitate. They also tend to see the non-Amish world as a place of threat and perdition, a belief largely justified and supported by their own history of being persecuted, and given a lively reality for contemporary American Amish by the use of an extensive and detailed martyrology, *The Bloody Theatre or Martyrs Mirror*, in which lively accounts of past martyrdoms, Amish and others, are given.[18] The non-Amish world is a place of violence, and the central element in Amish response to it is nonresistance. The Amish are pacifist, and they are not supposed to resist the violence they expect to be offered them by the non-Amish world – violence which is still today not infrequently offered them.

Any community that attempts, as the Amish do, total, comprehensive separation must have strongly-marked boundaries and some means of maintaining them. Both are evident in Amish life. It's very clear from a moment's glance, to both insiders and outsiders, who is Amish and who is not; and the community maintains harsh sanctions against those of its own who offend against its discipline, up to and including complete exclusion or banishment ("shunning"). The key temptation for Amish, and therefore the key matter to guard against, is worldliness: the desire for the goods and practices of the non-Amish world. Separatists like the Amish, in a context where they are the minority, must exercise constant vigilance.

This example, sketchily presented as it is, suggests that the recommendation and adoption of separatist attitudes toward the religiously alien (or, in the case canvassed, toward the alien in general) flows from two things. First, the particulars of the home religion, especially its doctrines and teachings; and second, a diagnosis of the situation in which the inhabitants of that religion find themselves. In the case of the Amish, it seems, there are doctrinal reasons for separation, reasons that make contact with the alien either dangerous or irrelevant. There are no corresponding positive reasons for reducing the strength of the separatist impulse: aliens are not, for instance, seen as possible converts, and no efforts are made in this direction. Second, the separatist community – the sect, as sociologists of religion will likely want to call it – will offer an account of the situation it finds itself in, an account that will affect the particulars of its separatist efforts. The rules and regulations governing Amish observance, for instance, are quite particular about which material elements of the alien culture must be shunned and which need not be; and this requires some continuing and growing knowledge of what the alien culture is doing (the telephone wasn't always an option, for instance; when it became so, the Amish had to decide what to do about it). The diagnosis offered of the local situation will also (as in the case of the Amish it does) typically flow from and depend upon particulars of the religious account of things offered by the home community.

Those who advocate total and comprehensive separation, like the Amish, will, as we've seen, think of themselves as self-sufficient (or at least as capable of being so) with respect to everything of central importance to their lives. The Amish seek material, social, emotional, and reproductive self-sufficiency. But more interestingly for our purposes, they also take themselves to have religious self-sufficiency. They need, religiously speaking, nothing that any religious alien might have to offer; if they did, of course, they could not think of themselves as religiously self-sufficient. This position, then, has direct implications for what such a community will typically think about the questions of truth and epistemic confidence, discussed respectively in chapters 2 and 3. On truth, such a community will adopt either exclusivism or closed inclusivism, and in either case will not be very interested in the question. And on the question of epistemic confidence, the preferred response will be that knowledge of diversity in religious assents has absolutely nothing to say about the degree of epistemic confidence with which the Amish should assent to their doctrines and teachings. If the non-Amish world really is a dark and dangerous place, swept away by the flood-tide of worldly passions, then the fact that some of those who live there assent to claims incompatible with what the Amish claim is hardly surprising and not very interesting. This is a clear instance of the move from a high degree of initial epistemic confidence in religious assents – coupled with the capacity of one's religious account to explain and predict diversity of assent – to a dismissal of any epistemic significance in the knowledge of diversity. It's a connection that is typical of separatist religions.

Are there nonreligious versions of separatism? Are the nonreligious likely to want or advocate total or partial separation from the religious alien? This occurs, of course. Agents of nations that profess themselves nonreligious sometimes refuse to recognize the religious status of groups that think of themselves as religious, and even go so far as to make some of their activities illegal. Some German courts in the 1980s and 1990s have, for instance, acted in this way toward the Church of Scientology. Such actions may go so far as to show, on the part of a professedly nonreligious state, a desire for total separation from at least some religions. And nonreligious individuals may also sometimes show such a desire for separation from all or some selected religious aliens. When this happens, it will be based on what are, structurally and functionally, the same kinds of reasons that inform religious separatism. Those wanting separation will offer an account of things according to which those from whom separation is desired are dangerous or to be hated or both. But it's probably true that desires for total, comprehensive separation like those evident among the Amish are less common among the nonreligious than among the religious. This is because it is easier for those who inhabit a form of life that seems to them comprehensive and of unsurpassable and central importance than for those who do not to come to think of their community as self-sufficient in all that matters – and this is, as we've seen, an important ingredient in separatist desires.

Philosophical assessment of separatism with respect to the religiously alien is in one way very easy and in another way impossibly difficult. There are, I think, no general conceptual criticisms to be made of the coherence of separatism; in this it differs from toleration. Separatism is entirely coherent on its face; this is the easy part of assessment. Whether it is defensible in any particular case will depend on the plausibility of the specifics of the religious account of things on which it rests. And since these specifics are uncountably many, this makes philosophical assessment extremely difficult. In the case of Amish separatism, it seems, effective criticism could only be mounted by looking at the theological frame that gives it sense and purchase. And this would mean the very challenging task of exploring and attempting to assess, among other things, what to say about the complex of theology and canon law expressed in the eighteen canons adopted at the Synod of Dort held in 1632, a confessional statement held in common by Amish and Mennonites.

Non-Amish Christians might think that some of these canons misunderstand what Christianity is about; and non-Christians might think the canons a tissue of falsehood and confusion. But there seems no reason to doubt that Amish separatism comports well with what the canons claim, and no easy way to resolve disputes of the kind mentioned. This fact should remind you of a theme that has come up several times before in this book: I mean the idea that resolution of the conceptual difficulties raised by knowledge of religious diversity is often possible only by deciding on the truth of some claims peculiar to particular religions. This is true of separatism as a set of attitudes and behaviors directed at the religious alien: you'll reject it if you reject the theology from which it is derived; you'll accept it if you accept that theology.

## 4.3   Conversion: Domesticating the Religious Alien

The desire to domesticate the alien, whether religious or not, is the desire to turn those who are not like you into your kin. This is an extraordinarily widespread human desire. Almost all of us would like those who are very different from us, whether in appearance, political conviction, aesthetic tastes, or modes of behavior – to be less different. Deep differences in any of the matters mentioned often make peaceful and neighborly coexistence difficult or impossible. If we live next door to one another and I like to spend my Saturday afternoons playing loud music on the sidewalk outside my house while I work on my car, whereas you like to spend your Saturdays in undisturbed tranquility reading the newspaper on your porch, we are likely to find the differences in our leisure habits productive of friction. And this is a trivial example of the kinds of difficulties that difference in habits, preferences, attitudes, and desires can create for harmonious coexistence.

By conversion you make those who were once alien into your kin: you domesticate them. Those who attempt to convert the alien are, we might say, evangelists; and what they do is to evangelize. These are terms from the lexicon of Christianity. The Greek word *euangelion* means "good message" or "good news," and it has traditionally been rendered into English as "gospel." *Euangelion* is thus the word rendered "gospel" in the titles of each of the four gospels; as a result it has also come to denote those particular works, but in its broader sense, it means the essential Christian message. An evangelist, therefore, in the Christian sense of the word, is someone who offers this message to others in the hope that they will come to accept it; this is what it means to evangelize. But as I shall use these terms, they'll be uprooted from this specifically Christian context and given a broader application. On my usage, an evangelist is anyone who wants to domesticate the alien, anyone who seeks the alien's conversion.

Conversion can never be complete. In this it differs from separation. You can desire total separation from the alien (even if you can't easily attain it), but since total conversion would require making the alien in every respect like the evangelist, it is not something that can coherently be desired, much less something obtainable in practice. Evangelists, then, always have something more limited than this in mind: they want to make the alien like them in some respects only. Perhaps I'd like to make you into a follower of the Chicago White Sox, a lover of the late novels of Henry James, or an admirer of Augustine's thought. But even if I'm an evangelist in these ways, I have no interest in making you into a clone of me, no interest in making you in every respect like me. Any such interest would be evidence of insanity.

Evangelistic desires are therefore always and necessarily limited in scope in the sense that they pick out only some respects in which the alien should be domesticated. But evangelists differ from one another in the scope of their evangelistic desires in another and more interesting way. Some evangelists want to convert all aliens to whatever it is they're evangelizing about; they are, we might say, comprehensive in their evangelistic desires, for there is no one who falls outside them. Other evangelists, though, aim their evangelism at a subset of possible recipients; their evangelism, we might say, is limited.

Most evangelism is of the latter, limited sort. I don't want to convert everyone to an appreciation of the aesthetic and moral merits of the late novels of Henry James; those who can't read at all and those who can't read English (the prose of James's late novels must lose badly in translation) are outside the scope of my evangelism in this respect. Similarly, I would like to turn Chicago Cubs supporters from their habits to a deep and positive appreciation of the merits of the White Sox; them I'd happily (though probably ineffectively) evangelize. But I don't think that my English relatives are appropriate recipients of evangelistic work about this matter: they mostly don't even know what baseball is, and so it would be at best premature to persuade them into an appreciation of the White Sox.

Some evangelism, though, is comprehensive; some evangelists think that all aliens (at least, all human ones) should be domesticated with respect to whatever they're evangelizing about. We'll see in a moment that religious evangelism is often like this, but it's not alone in being so. There are advocates of free-market capitalism who think that it would be good if everyone were converted to the gospel of the market. There are dietary evangelists who'd like everyone to believe in the gospel of a low-fat, high-fiber diet. And there are, certainly, commercial evangelists who'd very much like it if all human beings were converted to belief in the merits of, say, Pepsi-Cola, and were as a result to become regular consumers of it.

Desires to convert may also be differentiated by motive. Some evangelists are motivated principally by a passion to get people to cease to believe in or do something that seems, from the viewpoint of the evangelist, unambiguously and indubitably bad for them. They, we might say, are the scolds, the stop-it-or-else evangelists. A classic example is to be found in antismoking evangelists whose chief mission in life is to get others to stop using nicotine and by so doing to be domesticated, to join the home community of healthy nonusers of nicotine. Others, though, are motivated primarily by a desire to offer to those whom they evangelize something they take to be a great good, something that they hope the alien will adopt. They, we might say, are the bringers of gifts, the offerers of salvation. Peculiarly American instances of this motivation are to be found among those who are convinced they've found a universally applicable answer to some universal human question: Norman Vincent Peale's advocacy of the power of positive thinking was like this, as was Dale Carnegie's recipe for winning friends and influencing people, and as, today, are the endless promises spilling from the presses, the airwaves, and the electronic ether of salvation through better managing your money or your sex life or your weight. Evangelists of this sort aren't scolds so much as hucksters. Mixed cases of scolding and hucksterism are of course frequent. The scold will often have a positive promise behind her back; and the huckster will often attempt to convince you of the benefits of his product by letting you know, in grisly detail, what's wrong with the ones you're using now. Nonetheless, the scold and the huckster are easily recognizable as ideal types, and they show clearly that evangelists are not all motivated in just the same way.

Evangelists may also be distinguished by the methods they choose to adopt. There is a range of possibilities here. At one end of the scale lie those who choose compulsion as their method of choice. Domesticating the alien by compulsion will, in the extreme case, face the alien with a simple choice: become like us in the chosen respect (accept baptism, become an American citizen, renounce allegiance to Trotskyism, give up the idea that a free Tibet would be good), or be killed. There are less extreme sanctions, of course: the threat of violence or other damage may suffice. But whatever the sanctions, the underlying idea of the evangelist-by-compulsion remains the same: it is that the good of domesticating the alien outweighs all other goods with respect to that alien, up to and including the alien's life. Along with this goes the view that engagement of the alien's believing consent is not especially important; much more important will be the forcing of certain actions upon the alien. If, as I've already suggested in chapter 2, belief is largely involuntary, it will not be possible to produce it in someone by threat or use of force in any straightforwardly direct way; and if this is so, it's equally unlikely that evangelists who favor compulsion will be directly interested in it. They're more likely to want the performance of certain actions: a public profession of the view that Trotskyite ideas are heretical; a repudiation of the ideas and practices of the Ku Klux Klan . . . and so on.

The relation between forced action and belief, though, is complicated, and the thoughtful evangelist-by-compulsion will realize this. A forced action, especially one with powerful symbolic significance for the one upon whom it is forced, may over time have extremely significant effects upon cognitive life. The architects and prosecutors of the persecution of Christians in Japan in the seventeenth century understood this, at least if Shusaku Endo's riveting account (in his novel *Silence*) of the procedures and goals of these trials is anything to go by. Rodrigues, a Portuguese Catholic priest who is the protagonist in that novel, is compelled by his accusers and torturers initially only to do something – to trample on an image of Christ's face. The Japanese torturers tell him that they don't care how he understands this action and that they have no interest in what he takes himself to be assenting to in performing it. But they understand that if Rodrigues does trample on the image he will find it hard to avoid taking it as a symbol of apostasy, and that his action will, whether he likes it or not, have significant effects over time upon the ways in which he understands himself and his relations to the Christian faith – as it turns out to do. This is a classic case of evangelism-by-compulsion in a number of ways. First, its only interest in aliens has to do with their domestication; second, it focuses initially upon compelling action (utterance or other actions perceptible to the public); and third, it is aware of the complex relations between compelled action and believing assent over time, and is interested in manipulating these variables in such a way as to transform not only the public actions of those being evangelized, but also their assents.

Compulsion is not the only method favored by evangelists. Perhaps it is no longer the most common. At least equally common, certainly, is the method of persuasion. Here, ideally, evangelists threaten nothing and are interested from the beginning in gaining the freely-willed assent of those they evangelize. They may, like those who use compulsion, be primarily interested in the alien as one who might be domesticated; but there will be constraints and limits placed upon the methods thought appropriate to achieving this end, perhaps by the institutional situation in which the evangelism-by-persuasion is being done, or perhaps by the particulars of the convictions that prompt it. If, for instance, a lobbyist in Washington or London is concerned to evangelize the holders and exercisers of power in those places about the desirability of reducing the government's active part in the provision of health care to the people, she is likely to be constrained in what she can do by her institutional location. She will offer argument; she may offer bribes, so called or rhetorically concealed as gifts and tokens of appreciation; but she will at least behave as though she has interests in the alien (the elected representative who's a strong advocate of a nationalized health-care system, for example) that extend beyond his conversion to her line of thought. Similarly, an evangelist for the benefits of democracy may likely limit his evangelical persuasions to argument (renouncing bribery, flattery, and so on) because it is central to his view of things that what makes democracy good is precisely that it maximizes opportunities for reasoned argument, and that where such opportunities are maximized the right views will always, over time, come to be held by most people. On such a view it would make little sense to evangelize by anything other than argument; and it is normal that evangelists will be limited in the techniques they find it possible to use by the particulars of the view in the service of which they are evangelizing.

A final method likely to be used by evangelists is that of simple presentation. Here, while the goal (or at least the hope) is still domestication of the alien in some important respect or another, both compulsion and explicit persuasion are renounced. What the evangelist does instead is simply to present – to make evident – to the alien whatever it is she's interested in evangelizing about. Suppose it's the desirability of a new method of cultivating wheat. The evangelist would like all wheat-cultivators to adopt this method (which means she's engaged in limited evangelism: not everyone's a cultivator of wheat) and, thereby, to abandon the methods they're already using (so she's both a scold and a huckster, even though one who scolds the evils to which she's opposed and offers the goods in which she's interested without ever explicitly mentioning the disadvantages of the one or the benefits of the other). But she has no interest in compulsion (perhaps she holds ethical views that prohibit it), and she judges that wheat-cultivators are unlikely to respond well to active persuasion. So, convinced of her method's superiority, she plants her wheat, cultivates it as she sees fit, and waits for other wheat-cultivators to learn how much better her method is than theirs (perhaps it requires no pesticides and no machinery, and yet gives yields three times as good as what can be achieved by any other method), and so to beat a path to her door.

So far I've analyzed the desire to convert, to domesticate the alien, in general terms. I've suggested that evangelists may be differentiated according to the scope of their evangelistic desires (do they want to convert everyone or just some people?), according to the motives with which they do their work (are they scolds or hucksters?), and according to the methods they prefer (do they compel, persuade, or simply present?). This analysis can, as suggested by several of the examples so far offered, be applied much more broadly than to the question of religious aliens. But I'll now turn my attention specifically to the latter question – to the question, that is to say, of the kinds of evangelistic response to the religious alien most likely to be met with, and to some brief comment upon the problems and advantages of these kinds.

Are the nonreligious likely to desire the conversion of the religious (recall that for the nonreligious all religious people are religious aliens)? Are, that is, the nonreligious likely to behave toward the religious as evangelists? The answer is, of course, yes. Most commonly, the nonreligious will respond evangelistically when faced with a view belonging to some particular religion as to how people ought to behave which they find unacceptable. They may attempt to convince the alien of the undesirability or impropriety of holding such a view, and so become persuasive evangelists; they may attempt to compel, by law or other sanctions up to and including violence, the religious aliens who both hold and act upon such a view, to cease acting upon it (and perhaps in the long term to cease holding it – recall Rodrigues). Or, they may simply present another option, and hope that it will be sufficiently attractive to the religious aliens who need conversion that they will adopt it.

A case in point. Some religious people (Muslims and others) practice various forms of female genital mutilation, operations done on prepubescent girls with the goal of limiting (and so controlling) the sensual pleasure connected with female sexuality. Some, apparently, support this on what seem to them religious grounds, as a means of ensuring that female sexual desire and procreative capacity are used properly. They support it and perform it, this is to say, as part of the specifically religious account of things they offer. Many others, religious and nonreligious, find the practice morally abhorrent, and will try almost anything, beginning with persuasion and reaching at least up to the use of sanctions connected with national and international law, to prevent it. The opponents of female genital mutilation in this case are evangelists of the scolding kind: they judge a particular kind of religiously-approved behavior to be such that the alien ought to be persuaded – or, if persuasion fails, compelled – to abandon it. This kind of response by the nonreligious to religious aliens is common; other examples of it have already been canvassed (recall the United States government's use of force to prevent polygamy on the part of Latter-Day Saints).

Less common, but still sometimes met with, is a comprehensively evangelical response to religious aliens by the nonreligious. Underlying this response is a judgment by the nonreligious that, ideally, all those who inhabit religious forms of life should cease to do so – that, perhaps, it would be better for each religious individual to cease to be so, and that the world would be a better place were there no religious forms of life in it. Feminist theorists, for instance, sometimes argue that all women are damaged by being religious because inhabiting religious forms of life inevitably places them at the mercy of a dangerously patriarchal system, and does so in ways that can only prevent them from flourishing. Marxist theorists have sometimes argued that religious forms of life are so deeply intertwined with oppressively inegalitarian social structures that effective transformation of these structures requires abandonment of religion. And some supporters of democracy, especially in its peculiarly American form, try, evangelically, to persuade those who think of themselves as religious to understand this aspect of their lives as exclusively private and personal, as more like a taste for golf or flower-arranging than like habitation of a comprehensive, unsurpassable, and centrally important construal of the world.

Each of these approaches requires (or at least recommends) the abandonment of religion: the feminist critique requires this of all women, the Marxist critique of everyone without remainder, and the democratic critique, with more subtlety than the other two, also of everyone − but this time by appeal for a radically new understanding of what it is to be religious rather than by a straightforward appeal for abandonment. Recall the discussion of privatization in chapter 3: there I made the point that privatization (the reduction of religious claims to claims whose primary referent is the preferences of those who assent to or entertain them), is a tempting response to the epistemic pressure brought to bear by knowledge of diversity in religious assents. I also suggested in the course of that discussion that the extent to which this temptation is succumbed to is precisely the extent to which a religious account of things ceases to be offered. But here, in the context of a discussion of attempts by the nonreligious to domesticate the religious alien − to convert them from being religious to not being so − it is important to add that there is often a wholly evangelical fervor about the persuasions offered by the nonreligious to the religious on this matter. The example of the philosopher Richard Rorty will show this.

Rorty has claimed that he sees the secularization of public life as the "Enlightenment's main achievement," and the main job of intellectuals to be "getting our fellow citizens to rely less on tradition, and to be more willing to experiment with new customs and institutions."[19] This, then, is evangelism: Rorty's fellow-citizens who are wedded to tradition (especially religious tradition) are to be domesticated, which is to say made like Rorty and others who are not so wedded. It is characteristic of intellectuals, says Rorty, that they "do not find religion what [William] James called a 'live, forced and momentous option',"[20] and that they are happy with the Jeffersonian compromise, which privatized religion and made it seem in bad taste to bring it into public discussion. Given this view, Rorty thinks that intellectuals should want the claims of religion "to be pushed back still further,"[21] and that those who want to use their religion as the basis and frame for their political engagements ought not so to want. Instead, he says, our religious convictions, if we have them, should be treated like our sexual habits or our aesthetic tastes: they should be understood as non-trivial but also as private, nonpolitical. This means that religious convictions – what I've been calling assents understood by those who make them to be central to a religious form of life – can have no place in the public life of a Jeffersonian democracy, which is to say that they can have no place in the public life of the United States at the beginning of the twenty-first century. If they are given such a place, thinks Rorty, democracy will prove unsustainable.[22]

Rorty further thinks that when religious people want to offer arguments about matters of public policy (about the desirability and legality of abortion, or female genital mutilation, or capital punishment, or the use of tax revenues for germ-warfare research), they are free to do so, but must do so by dropping any reference to the source of the arguments, which is to say by dropping any reference to the fact that positions on these matters will typically seem to religious people to be derived from the religious form of life they inhabit. "This omission," he says, "seems a reasonable price to pay for religious liberty."[23] This means that religious people cannot, if Rorty's prescriptions are followed, continue to understand their religious form of life as providing them with positions and arguments relevant to the ordering of public life in a Jeffersonian democracy. Or, if they do continue so to think, they must pretend they don't by excising all reference to their religion when they advocate positions in public policy or make arguments relevant to such positions. On Rorty's view, the extent to which religious people refuse to make this adjustment is precisely the extent to which they cease to have a voice that ought to be heard in the deliberations that produce public-policy decisions in a Jeffersonian democracy. This leaves religious people who don't want to make this adjustment (people for whom their religion seems to them to require more of them than does their taste for origami) with only three options. The first is conversion: agreement with Rorty that religious convictions must be privatized. The second is silence and withdrawal from the public sphere (the Amish option, discussed above under the heading of separation). And the third is pretence: choosing self-censorship as a necessary element of engagement in public debate, or (what is the effective equivalent) choosing to translate (and so to misrepresent) the nature of one's convictions as a religious person when engaging in argument with the nonreligious.

This brief discussion of Rorty's position is intended only to show that there are nonreligious people whose chief attitude to the religious alien is that of the evangelist. There are, of course, also many inhabitants of religious forms of life whose response to the religious alien is motivated largely by the desire to convert. This comes naturally to many (though by no means to all) inhabitants of religious forms of life because of the characteristics of those forms of life. They are, I've suggested, seen by those who inhabit them as comprehensive, unsurpassable, and of central importance to the answering of life's questions. It will be easy, then, for them also to be seen as having a universal bearing, as being relevant to all people; it will also be easy for them to be seen as offering something of great benefit to all — perhaps as communicating what God wants of all people, or as explaining how to live if the endless round of suffering, rebirth, and redeath is to be avoided. If your religion does seem like this to you — universally relevant and universally beneficial — then you're very likely to find evangelism attractive as an attitude to the religious alien.

You may even find that the particulars of your religious form of life require this attitude of you. This has certainly been true for many Christians, Buddhists, and Muslims. These are the world's great missionary religions; each of them has as a central part of its self-understanding the idea that it would be good for everyone to know of this form of life, and that it would be good for all to enter it. This places an imperative upon Buddhists and Christians and Muslims to do what they can to make it possible for these things to happen; and this is why Buddhism, for example, has spread from its beginnings in India to become known virtually everywhere, and has struck deep roots in most of Asia. It is also why Christianity now counts about one-fifth of the world's population among its (at least notional) adherents, and why Islam is entrenched from Indonesia to Morocco and is perhaps the fastest-growing of these three religions. Each of these traditions espouses conversion as a central element (though never as the only element) in its response to the religious alien.

But it is also true that the particulars of a religious form of life may not suggest that domestication of the alien is a good thing. We've already seen that there are religious forms of life whose response to the religious alien is dominated by the desire for separation, or, still more radically, for isolation, rather than for conversion. The Amish are not alone in this. Many Jews have a similar response, partly conditioned by a long experience of persecution by aliens of all sorts (including Christians), but partly conditioned also by the specifics of their account of things. This account focuses upon the free agency of God in choosing or electing the Jews from among all the peoples of the world; as a result it does not (usually) focus upon the desirability of non-Jews becoming Jewish. If this happens it may be welcomed; but seeking it and trying to make it happen has not histori-cally been a central part of how Jews understand themselves. Hindus also have not been much interested in converting the religious alien, mostly because (to over-simplify somewhat) being Hindu has been understood to be a matter of birth to an Indian family (usually in India), and so the idea of conversion (at least in this life – a rebirth in which entry into a Hindu form of life is possible may always be hoped for) makes little sense. Reli-gious forms of life will not, then, always issue in a desire for conversion. As always, almost everything will depend upon the particulars of the form of life.

There are connections between the view that domestication is the right thing to do with (or to) religious aliens, and particular views about truth and epistemic confidence. On the question of truth, a highly evangelistic religion is likely to be either exclusivist or an advocate of closed inclu-sivism. It is less likely (though possible) that it might be an advocate of open inclusivism – the view, recall, that alien religions might teach reli-giously-significant truths not yet known to the home religion. This is because a religion that did attempt to combine a strongly evangelical approach to the religious alien with open inclusivism on truth would run the risk of not learning some truths that it needed to know by extin-guishing the religion that taught these truths. This danger could be addressed by including an advocacy of open inclusivism in attempts at con-version – which is to say, by making dialogue an element in the process of conversion; but there will always be a tension if open inclusivism and the desire for conversion are combined.

There are complex relations between an evangelical approach to the religious alien and views as to the effect that knowledge of diversity in religious assent does or should have upon epistemic confidence. It would perhaps be natural to expect that inhabitants of an evangelical religion will not be epistemically troubled by their coming to know that aliens give assent to claims incompatible with those of the home religion. After all, if the central attitude to religious aliens is the desire to domesticate them, this will usually imply that those with such a desire take themselves to be able to offer something of great value to the alien; it does not immedi-ately suggest that they are likely to be troubled by coming to know that the assents of the alien are incompatible with theirs. Indeed, this may be expected; the desire to convert is often closely linked with the view that those who have not (yet) been domesticated are in some way confused, lost, or lacking; and the discovery of diversity in assent may be taken as confirming evidence of their need for conversion. But it is also possible that the desire to convert may be a reaction to perceived threat. In an extreme case, it could be an integral part of a desire to extinguish the troubling other, to remove by domestication or by death those who create epistemic difficulties by their very presence. Again, particular cases will have to be examined to see how the connections might go.

It remains to ask whether there are any in-principle objections that might be brought against the desire to domesticate the religious alien. Many think that there are. Missionary activity, certainly when it uses the tools of persuasion or compulsion, is often taken to be a paradigm case of intolerant and unacceptable behavior, especially by those who have already decided that religious identity is a matter of choice and preference, of the same kind as tastes in ice-cream, sexual behavior, or music. But here it is important to distinguish between the desire to domesticate the religious alien (which we have seen to be had by some religious as well as by some nonreligious people), on the one hand, and certain methods used in its service, on the other. It's possible to offer arguments against, for example, the use of violence (or the threat of violence) as a tool of conversion, without thereby thinking that there's necessarily anything wrong with the desire to convert as such.

Indeed, it's difficult to see what kind of argument might be brought either against having such a desire or against acting upon it. If you believe that a particular behavior is likely to cause deep and irreversible damage to all who engage in it, and if you also would like to prevent such damage wherever you can, then you're likely to harbor evangelistic desires toward those who (through ignorance or sin or sheer cussedness) don't share your views about the behavior in question. And, given that you have such desires and are not prevented from acting upon them, some form of evangelistic activity will (and should) follow. Perhaps, if the behavior in question is driving when drunk, you'll found a missionary organization dedicated to evangelism-by-persuasion on this matter. If it's legalized killing of con- victed criminals, you may do the same on that matter. And so forth. You may of course be wrong in your convictions about the harms produced by the behavior in question; and many of those you attempt to convert may not be converted. But it's hard to see what sort of argument might yield the conclusion that all instances of such behavior ought to be ruled out in principle. The moral and practical uneasiness that many contem- porary Americans and Europeans have about specifically religious attempts at conversion are usually derived directly from a sense that religious belief and behavior is a private matter of taste, and that as a result attempts to alter it from without are either themselves in bad taste, or are evidence of irrationality on the part of those engaging in them. You'd find it odd, possibly even evidence of my insanity, if I knocked on your door and attempted to convert you from playing tennis to playing squash or founded an organization dedicated to spreading the word about the benefits of supporting the Notre Dame football team. You might find attempts at religious evangelism equally odd. But if you do it is probably because you've come to understand religious conviction and behavior as Richard Rorty would have you understand it; and there is no pressing reason so to understand it.

I would go further. It's likely the case that both the desire to domesticate the alien and the performance of some actions implied by such a desire, is an element of the human affective and cognitive condition that is very difficult to check or constrain. If you examine your own beliefs and attitudes, you'll certainly find that some of them are best understood as such desires. This is most obvious for parents; much of what we do in the way of raising children is best understood as a form of missionary activity, an attempt to domesticate (to make in important respects like us) the excessively alien creatures we've brought into the world. But it's also true for friends (you'd usually try to persuade your friend to do something you're sure would be very good for her), and often for fellowcitizens (much of the democratic process is about evangelism-by-persuasion). So not only is there no in-principle problem with the desire to domesticate the alien; such desires are an intrinsic part of the human condition. This is of course perfectly compatible with there being deep problems with – and good arguments against – particular instances of activity aimed at such domestication: activity, for instance, that uses violence or the threat of violence. It is compatible, as well, with the view that not all religions require this attitude of their inhabitants with respect to religious aliens. Here too, everything will depend upon the particulars of the religion in question.

The tolerationist, separatist, and conversionist attitudes discussed so far in this chapter are not mutually exclusive. They'll most often be found in impure or mixed forms, associated one with another in complicated ways. It's possible, for instance, to have noncomprehensive desires to domesticate the alien (to think, that is, that only some aliens ought to be domesticated) coupled with tolerationist attitudes toward others. It's possible to be largely separatist, but with some tolerationist or conversionist exceptions. And so on. The ideal types sketched above will rarely be found. Attention to a particular case will show how complex the connections among them can be.


## 4.4   Christian Evangelism

In December 1990, in the thirteenth year of his papacy, John Paul II issued an encyclical letter called *Redemptoris Missio* [Mission of the Redeemer], whose central topic is the urgency and importance of Christian missionary activity, of what I've been calling the desire to domesticate the alien – and indeed not just the alien but, finally, everyone. This document is representative of much in Christian thinking about the topic of this chapter (much that is held in common, for example, by Protestant, Catholic, and Orthodox Christians), and so it will serve both as an almost ideal-typical instance of Christian thought about attitudes and actions aimed at the religious alien, but also as an instance of what it is like to think about this matter from within the bounds of a particular set of religious commitments.

*Redemptoris Missio* emphasizes that "the missionary thrust . . . belongs to the very nature of the Christian life."[24] The desire to domesticate the alien is not a peripheral matter for Christians; it is, rather, a central element in the Christian account of things, one with biblical roots and a long history. All Christians are called upon to evangelize, to spread the Christian message to those who do not yet assent to or accept its central claims; and one of the indexes of the Church's vitality is the extent to which it does this.[25] These are claims about what the particulars of the Christian form of life requires of those who inhabit it; and as my analysis in this chapter has suggested will typically be the case, they are grounded upon other, broader claims about the nature of human beings and the environment in which we find ourselves. It is because Christians understand the world to be a certain way and human beings to be of a certain sort that they think of themselves as bound to missionary activity, to the desire to domesticate the alien. If the question is "Why then should there be missionary activity?,"[26] the answer must be in terms of fundamental Christian convictions about the world and human beings, and these *Redemptoris Missio* provides.

The most fundamental of these convictions is about Jesus of Nazareth. For Christians, this man is the second person of the triune God, the Son of God, and his life, death, and resurrection is of central importance to all human beings, whether they know it or not. It is because of their understanding of and faith in these facts (as they seem to Christians and as they are presented in *Redemptoris Missio*), and because of the deeply positive transformation that such understanding and faith brings about in those who have it, that the desire to domesticate the alien is so important for Christians. They think of themselves as knowing in part (but more fully than anyone else – recall the discussion of inclusivism in chapter 2) what everyone ought to know; and they are motivated and impelled by these convictions to communicate their convictions and to increase the number of those who share them.[27] A very substantial part of *Redemptoris Missio* is devoted to exploration and explanation of these convictions about Jesus Christ; the details of this analysis lie outside the scope of this discussion (to enter upon them would be to engage in Christian theology), but it can be said that the upshot of the document's analysis is to bring into close connection the idea of Jesus Christ as witness to (and himself inaugurator of) God's Kingdom with the idea of the community of Christians (the church, the body of Christ) as itself God's most explicit witness on earth to the bringing about of the Kingdom.[28] Christ and Church are therefore linked symbiotically; and if the church is to play its proper role in witnessing to Christ and furthering the coming of the Kingdom, it must do so by helping each of its members to understand themselves as evangelists.

The evangelism of Christians, on this understanding, is universal in scope,[29] and is motivated largely by a desire to share something that its possessors regard as an unmixed good (what I called above the huckster's motivation), rather than by the scold's motivation to get aliens to stop their bad habits. But Christian evangelism as presented in *Redemptoris Missio* rejects compulsion as a method:[30] faith cannot in fact be compelled, and such compulsion ought not to be attempted.[31] Christian evangelism is interested in the alien's free acceptance, not in his compelled conversion. Evangelism is also constrained by a conviction that the Holy Spirit's activity is not found only among Christians. Religious aliens are also inspired by the Spirit to believe and speak truth,[32] and this means that deep respect for what religious aliens do and say must always inform Christian evangelism.

The document mentions both persuasion (using the example of Paul's speeches in Lystra and Athens described in Acts 14 and 17) and presentation as desirable evangelistic methods.[33] Christians should offer aliens explicit witness to the Christian Gospel, an explicit witness – a proclamation – that may in certain contexts include or require persuasive argument.[34] But they should also witness by means of "a way of life that shines out to others"[35] – which means by simply showing the alien how Christians live, what a Christian way of life comes to.[36] Witness of this kind finds its fulfilment and ideal in martyrdom, the acceptance of death as a means of bearing witness to faith.[37] Both kinds of witness have conversion as their final aim, and this is understood to mean "accepting, by a personal decision, the saving sovereignty of Christ and becoming his disciple."[38]

Proclamation, persuasion, and presentation may be combined in many ways, according to *Redemptoris Missio*. Dialogue with the religious alien, while not itself directly aimed at conversion, can be understood as a kind of proclamation. This is because in sincere dialogue Christians necessarily present themselves as such, being explicit about what they believe and hope for. Dialogue can therefore properly be seen as part of witness-by-presentation.[39] The use of argument to persuade may also be an element in witness-by-presentation, since if it is done with due attention to the love and esteem generally required in all Christians' interactions with religious aliens,[40] it shows, in part, what a properly Christian life is like.

John Paul emphasizes that it would be a mistake to think of Christian missionary activity principally in terms of technique, as though its success could be assured by finding just the right way to do it. This would be a mistake because human beings are not the chief agents in bringing about conversion, even though their work is indispensable to it. God – in the person of the Holy Spirit – is the main agent of missionary activity,[41] and it is always God who converts, not human beings. Here too, then, Christian understanding of how to think about and respond to the religious alien is constrained and shaped by more fundamental Christian assents.

Christian attitudes and responses to religious aliens are also governed and controlled by Christian convictions that have nothing specifically to do with aliens. As *Redemptoris Missio* says, love is the "driving force of all mission,"[42] and serves as the sole criterion of what should and should not be done with or to the religious alien. But love is also the sole criterion of what should and should not be done with or to anyone at all. Its applicability to the religious alien is, then, simply an instance of a much broader and more fundamental Christian understanding of how human beings as such should be treated.[43] And in this it is typical of religious understandings of how religious aliens should be treated – that is, treatment of aliens will be affected by religious convictions about how humans in general should be treated.

How might such an understanding of properly Christian attitudes to the religious alien be critically assessed? In two significantly different ways.

First, by Christians. Questions and criticisms might be brought forward by other Christians. They might think, for instance, that some of the theological points emphasized by John Paul II are inadequate or mistaken as interpretations of Christianity. Some Christians think that Christianity need not be centered upon Jesus Christ in the way that *Redemptoris Missio* suggests, because what is of central importance to Christianity (God, the coming of the Kingdom, the establishment of peace and justice on earth) can be understood, proclaimed, and argued for without making Christ's place in it as central as *Redemptoris Missio* does. Those who take such a position will be likely to downplay the significance of Christ-centered proclamation or argument by Christians directed at the religious alien, and to emphasize the importance of evangelism-by-presentation. They may even interpret Christian evangelism in such a way as to remove its interest in domesticating the religious alien and to replace it with an interest in being tolerant of and learning to collaborate with the religious alien. Moves of this sort require fairly drastic and deep-going revisions in Christian understandings of God, especially with respect to the understanding of God as triune and Jesus of Nazareth as the second person of the trinity. But such discussions will in any case be intra-Christian ones.

Second, objections may be brought by non-Christians. These may call into question the theological underpinnings of the position, as also would the intra-Christian objections. Debate would likely proceed rather differently in this case, though, since there would be less in common upon the basis of which argument could usefully proceed. Nonchristians (religious or otherwise) are, however, not likely to be very interested in specifically Christian convictions of the kind mentioned. They're more likely to object to the desire to domesticate the alien as such, and to do so in broadly ethical grounds. I've already suggested that objections of that kind are unlikely to get very far, in part because they're almost certain to assume (without demonstrating) the falsehood of one or another key Christian conviction (about God or Jesus or the rest of us humans), and in part because it is almost certainly the case that some versions of the desire to domesticate the alien are unavoidable — and if unavoidable, not reasonably argued against in principle.

The upshot is that any rejection of the Christian view of how to think about and behave toward the religious alien just expounded requires rejection of the related complex set of convictions upon which it is founded and from which it is derived. The same will be true of any other religious view of the matters treated in this chapter.

## NOTES

1   John Courtney Murray, *Religious Liberty: Catholic Struggles with Pluralism*, ed. J. Leon Hooper (Louisville. Kentucky: Westminster/John Knox, 1993), p. 150.

2   There are important differences in the substance of what is argued in these two works, but they are not such as to affect the discussion that follows. I'll quote the versions contained in David Wootton, ed., *Political Writings of John Locke* (New York: Mentor, 1993).

3   Ibid., p. 393.

4   Ibid., p. 187.

5   Ibid., p. 396.

6   Ibid., p. 189.

7   Ibid., pp. 418–20.

8   Ibid., p. 390.

9   Ibid., pp. 404–5.

10  Ibid., p. 403.

11  Ibid., p. 197.

12  Ibid., p. 198.

13  Ibid.

14  Ibid., pp. 200–2.

15  Ibid., p. 415.

16  Ibid.

17  José Ignacio Cabezón, ed., *The Bodhgaya Interviews* (Ithaca, New York: Snow Lion, 1988), pp. 38–9.

18  *Bloody Theater: Or, Martyrs Mirror of the Defenseless Christians*, compiled by Thieleman J. van Braght, trans. Joseph F. Sohm (Scottsdale, Pennsylvania: Herald Press, 1972).

19  Richard Rorty, "Religion as Conversation-Stopper," *Common Knowledge* 3 (1994), pp. 1–6, at p. 1.

20  Ibid., p. 2.

21  Ibid.

22  Ibid., p. 3.

23  Ibid., p. 5.

24  *Redemptoris Missio* §1.3.

25  Ibid., §2.3, §11.3.

26  Ibid., §4.3, §11.3.

27  Ibid., §7.1.

28  Ibid., §§17–18.

29   Ibid., §31.1.
30   Ibid., §§8.1–8.3.
31   Ibid., §39.1.
32   Ibid., §§27–8.
33   Ibid., §§25–6.
34   Ibid., §44.
35   Ibid., §26.2.
36   Ibid., §42.
37   Ibid., §45.4.
38   Ibid., §46.2.
39   Ibid., §55.
40   Ibid., §44.3.
41   Ibid., §30.1.
42   Ibid., §60.4.
43   Ibid., §44.3.

# CHAPTER 5

# The Question of Salvation

The fundamental question about salvation is: What is the proper end of human beings? Putting the question in this way plays upon two of the meanings of "end" in English: end as cessation, the point at which a process ceases (the reign of George VI of England ended, in this sense, in 1952); and end as that toward which a process aims, its proper goal or purpose (the end of education in this sense – it might controversially be said – is the formation of character). If things go as they should, a process may end at the same point in both senses: perhaps my education will cease (end in the first sense) just when my character is formed (end in the second sense). A proper end, though, cannot be a simple cessation. It is, rather, a culmination that has achieved a purpose, an event or state of affairs that marks the completion of what some process was for. "Proper end," then, is a phrase that marks what philosophers would call a teleological idea, an idea that makes unavoidable reference to the *telos* (a Greek word meaning, principally, end in the second sense, end as purpose) of that to which it is applied.

On this understanding of the phrase "proper end," to ask how humans may realize their proper end is to assume that human life ought to be understood teleologically – and in the special sense of having a single, universally relevant purpose or goal. It is then to focus attention upon the question of how this purpose is to be realized. It is, in other words, to ask about how to get what all humans should want if they know what's good for them.

I'll adopt "salvation" as a shorthand term for the end (goal, purpose) that all of us should want. Although this term does have a specifically Christian meaning and use, I shall not intend that particular meaning unless I explicitly signal it. Rather, I'll use "salvation" abstractly to pick out the idea of a universal end, an end applicable to everyone, an end that everyone should want. I'll also use the term to pick out tokens of this type of idea, which is to say particular ideas about what this end is; but when I do this, the term will require a modifying adjective ("Buddhist salvation," "Islamic salvation") in order to indicate which particular ideas about what everyone should want are in play.

Some think that there is no salvation, no single end of human life that everyone should want. Others, perhaps, think that there is, but only in the first sense of end, so that the proper end of human life is understood simply as its cessation, its coming to a halt with death. These views will be found more commonly among the nonreligious than the religious. Inhabitants of religious forms of life typically do think that salvation is real and a real possibility, that it is what their form of life prescribes, and that inhabiting this form of life makes its attainment possible. Christians, for example, might think that the end in question is the love and service of God here below, and, after the resurrection of the body, the beatific vision. Attaining these ends is what it means to gain salvation, to be saved. Some Christians also think that you can't attain these ends unless you've been a Christian, an explicit follower and worshipper of Jesus Christ, prior to death. And Buddhists, to take a different example, tend to think that the end in question is the attainment of Nirvana, which is the end of the cycle of redeath and rebirth together with the suffering that accompanies it. Attaining these ends is what it means to be liberated or awakened. And some Buddhists also think that you can't attain these ends until you gain explicit and correct understanding of Buddhist doctrine, and engage in the mode of life commended by that doctrine.

Not all religions hold such views. Some, perhaps, claim that the salvation prescribed by their doctrine has no universal applicability or interest, that its attainment is restricted to those who inhabit the home religion, and that religious aliens should neither want nor seek it because it has no significance or benefit for them. Views of this sort tend to go with the making of deep distinctions between religious kin and religious aliens, distinctions analogous to those between species. If your religious kin are so deeply different from religious aliens that no serious intercourse is possible, if they are in some profound sense constituted differently, then it may seem to make about as much sense to postulate a single, universally relevant end for all humans as it does to postulate a single ideal environment for all mammals. But views of this sort are atypical. Most religions do envisage a single proper end for all humans, and it is this fact that raises in most pointed fashion the philosophical questions to be treated in this chapter.

The purpose of the discussion in this chapter is not to resolve the question of whether there is salvation for humans; much less is it to offer arguments about how, substantively, it ought to be understood. There are no arguments about these matters likely to convince everyone; and Christians, at least, have good theological reasons for thinking that there ought not to be, that a properly Christian understanding of and conviction about salvation and the proper means of getting it is not to be had or communicated by the offering of argument. This chapter is intended, instead, as an exploration of the most common and interesting ways of thinking about salvation in the light of religious diversity. Two families of questions are of special importance here. The first asks about the means by which we humans realize our proper end; the second asks which among us realizes that end. The two families of questions are related, obviously: what you think about how we realize our proper end will have an effect upon what you think about who in fact realizes that end, just as what you think about the second matter will have its effects upon what you think about the first. But even though there are close relations between the two families of questions, they are nevertheless conceptually distinct in much the same way that questions about how to get to be a good baseball player are conceptually distinct from questions about who gets to play the game. I'll treat the two families separately in the discussion that follows, but first some clarification of just what's being asked within each family will be useful.

Questions about the means proper to salvation – about how it's to be had – are especially relevant to the purposes of this book because discussions of these questions are most often carried on in the context of thought about religious diversity. This is because, for religious people, knowledge of the facts of religious diversity often sharpens these questions into an almost unbearably pointed form and forces concentrated thought about them. The question of salvation is often, for religious people, the most important question there is or could be. It is existentially important because it has to do with the proper end of the life of the person asking it, with what that life is most fundamentally and comprehensively for. And it is conceptually and ethically important because it has to do with the proper ends of all people, including not only one's religious kin but also the religious alien.

Religious people often find, then, that coming to know about religious diversity forces upon them the question of what inhabiting the home community has to do with getting saved, together with the related question of what inhabiting alien communities has to do with it. Some religious people think that inhabiting the home community is necessary for salvation, which is to say that if you don't inhabit the home religion you won't be able to get saved. On this view, inhabiting the home religion won't guarantee salvation; it's just indispensable for salvation, rather as having your eighteenth birthday won't guarantee having your twenty-first but is certainly indispensable for it. Others think that inhabiting the home religion is sufficient for salvation. On this view, inhabiting the home religion assures you of salvation – though there may be other ways to get saved as well. On this view, inhabiting the home religion is related to salvation much as being born on US soil is related to being a US citizen: the one entails the other. And the analogy will go further: being born on US soil isn't the only way to become a US citizen (you can be naturalized if foreign-born to non-US parents; or you are a citizen at birth if foreign-born to US parents). Yet others say that inhabiting the home religion is both necessary and sufficient for attaining salvation. On this view, if you inhabit the home religion, then not only will you attain salvation by doing so, but there's no other way to do it. Views of this sort link membership in the home religion and the attainment of salvation very tightly indeed, as tightly as being a member of the NBA's championship team in a particular year and receiving a championship ring for that year. A final view makes inhabiting the home religion neither necessary nor sufficient for salvation: perhaps salvation is thought not to have much to do with belonging to the home religion, much as weighing less than Bill Clinton has nothing much to do with belonging to the human race – being human is neither required for nor guarantees weighing less than Bill Clinton.

These are schematic views about what inhabiting the home community has to do with salvation. But in thinking about this question, religious people often think also about what membership in alien communities has to do with it. They consider, that is, not only whether inhabiting the home community is necessary, sufficient, both, or neither, for getting saved; they ask also whether inhabiting some (all? any particular?) alien religion is useful, sufficient, or irrelevant for getting saved. It has become traditional to distinguish three kinds of answers to this family of questions, each with its characteristic strengths and weaknesses. They are pluralism, exclusivism, and inclusivism, each to be treated separately below.

The second large family of questions about salvation has to do, recall, not so much with how you get saved as with who gets saved. What you think about this latter question will inevitably be connected with what you think about the effectiveness of belonging to the home religion (or to some alien religion) as a means of attaining salvation; but it is not the same question. Asking who is saved is asking the general question of what portion of the human race will attain its proper end; it may also be asking about the marks or characteristics of those who belong to that portion. When it does this latter thing, it approaches very closely to the question about the effectiveness of particular religious identities, for the marks in question will often be taken to be precisely those given by belonging to the home religion. I'll discuss the two main kinds of answers to the question of who is saved under the headings of universalism and restrictivism. But first to the three kinds of answers to the question of how we are saved, of what belonging to the home religion has to do with it.

## 5.1   Pluralism

At the most formal level pluralism says that belonging to the home religion bears the same relation to the attainment of salvation as does belonging to any alien religion. Most often, perhaps, pluralists will add to this the view that the relation in question is one of sufficiency, which is to say that belonging to any religion (with appropriate qualifiers about sincerity and such things) will guarantee you salvation. No pluralist, of course, can think that belonging to any particular religion is necessary for salvation, though they may certainly think that belonging to some religion or other is necessary. An upshot of all forms of pluralism with respect to salvation is that no benefit, so far as the attainment of salvation is concerned, is provided by belonging to one religious form of life rather than another. This is the central intuition in pluralistic responses to the question of salvation; it is most often the intuition that pluralistic responses are designed to enshrine.

Pluralism as formally stated in the preceding paragraph could theoretically be held in negative forms, according to which belonging to the home (or any) religion has no (or very little) causal or statistical connection with the attainment of salvation. Pluralism of this sort says that if you do attain salvation (however it may be understood) the fact that you do is not caused by, and may have little or nothing to do with, the fact that you are religious. Perhaps God's salvifically-effective grace or the Buddha's salvifically-effective action is not a respecter of religious identity, and so Christians and Buddhists are saved not because they are Christian or

Buddhist but because God (or the Buddha) decides for reasons unknown that they should be saved. But such negative forms of the pluralistic view are unlikely to be terribly attractive to religious people, for they sever the connection between being religious and attaining salvation. This will seem odd to religious people because, as we've seen, it is typically the case that religions offer an account of what salvation is and commend a mode of life that comports well with it. And so it will seem counterintuitive to say that knowing what the proper end of human life is and attempting a mode of life that comports well with such knowledge has nothing at all to do, causally or otherwise, with attaining that end. And this is just what the negative forms of the pluralistic view seem to say. Negative forms of pluralism are thus more likely to satisfy the nonreligious than the religious. But even among the nonreligious it does not seem that negative pluralism is widely held.

Pluralism can also be held in positive forms. These forms of the view affirm that there is a positive (usually, but not necessarily, causal) connection between belonging to the home religion and attaining salvation. And, because of the parity-claim intrinsic to the pluralistic answer to our question, it will also have to be said that whatever this connection is, just the same one holds between belonging to any alien religion and attaining salvation. Insofar as a pluralistic response proves attractive to religious people, it is likely to do so in a positive form. But even in such forms the pluralistic response raises immediate problems for many religious people. Such problems usually have to do with the element of unsurpassability in religious accounts of things. If you're religious, the account of things given to you by the form of religious life to which you belong will seem to you comprehensive, of central importance, and unsurpassable. This last characteristic (recall the discussion in chapter 1) is likely to lead you to be suspicious of claims that other forms of life can be placed on a par with yours with respect to effectiveness in making salvation possible. Such suspicions tend to be deepened when religious people come to know something of the particulars of religious diversity, for then it comes to be known that, at least on the face of things, there is deep incompatibility among the teachings and doctrines of different religions. How, then, can it be that belonging to any one of them is as effective as belonging to any other as a means of attaining salvation?

Doubts like these about the pluralistic response (positive or negative) to the question of salvation explain why few religions have taught it as the proper position to take. But this is not by itself to say that it can't coherently be taught. And since the response enjoys a higher profile in our time among some who call themselves Christian (it has no such profile among inhabitants of most other religions) than it has at most times in the past, and since it also raises some nice philosophical difficulties (in some respects analogous to those discussed in section 2.4), it will be useful to expound and discuss a particular version of it here.

As with the discussion of broadly Kantian views about religious truth in the context of religious diversity, I choose John Hick as my contemporary exponent of a pluralistic response (or at least a response fairly close to pluralism) to the question of salvation. What Hick thinks about salvation is closely tied to what he thinks about truth, and you should have the discussion of section 2.4 in mind as you read what follows.

Hick's understanding of the term "salvation" is like the one in play here in being detached from its specifically Christian connotations. But it is unlike the one in play here in being substantive rather than purely formal. Hick means by salvation "the transformation of human existence from self-centeredness to a new orientation, centered in the divine Reality,"[1] and this claims a particular content for salvation. What we are meant for, that at which we aim, according to this understanding, is to be centered upon something ("the divine Reality," or more often in Hick's recent work just "Reality") other than ourselves. Note the simple problem of vagueness. By contrast, the understanding of salvation in play in this book is formal in the sense that it refers only to whatever is taken by any religion to be the proper end of human life. This distinction – between a substantive (even if attenuatedly so) understanding of salvation and a strictly formal one – does, as we shall soon see, make a difference.

Hick's pluralistic interpretation of salvation leads him to see the question about salvation posed in this chapter as one of fact, one that can be answered (in theory if not easily in practice) by empirical observation of what belonging to particular religions in fact seems to do to people. This is because he thinks that understanding salvation as a transformation from self- to Reality-centeredness should have effects "upon the moral and spiritual quality of a human personality"[2] – effects such as making people kind, generous, sacrificial of their own interests for those of others. These effects should also be predictable (we should know what to expect) and discoverable (we should be able to find them). If all this is correct, it then becomes a matter of investigation: we should go and look closely at Buddhists, Muslims, Hindus, Christians, and so forth, and see to what extent these effects are evident in their lives. But this raises the obvious question: how do we get to know what these effects are? Isn't it likely, for example, that the moral and spiritual qualities thought by Christians to be evidence of transformation produced by being a good Christian will be different from those thought by Buddhists to be evidence of transformation produced by being a good Buddhist? And isn't it likely that both will be different from the moral and spiritual qualities thought by members of Aum Shinrikyo (the group that released nerve gas into the Tokyo subway system in 1995) to be evidence of transformation produced by being a faithful member of that community? And if there are indeed such differences, how will Hick's criterion be usefully applicable without pre-judgment of just the issue it is meant to resolve?

Hick's answer is that "at the level of their most basic moral insights the great traditions use a common criterion . . . they agree in giving a central and normative role to the unselfish regard for others that we call love or compassion."[3] If this descriptive claim is right, and if it is possible to decide which observable patterns of behavior are likely to result from elevating love/compassion in this manner – whether these patterns are looked for on an individual or on a broader socio-cultural level – then Hick will have the beginnings of what he needs to carry out the empirical program of assessing the salvific effectiveness of various religions.

Hick is clear about the difficulties involved in assessing whether, for instance, Buddhists are typically more loving than Christians; or whether the social forms that have developed in close connection with Christianity are more or less compassionate and just than those that have developed in close connection with Islam. But he sees these only as practical difficulties; and he claims that what unsystematic and anecdotal information we have about these things should lead us to conclude that "so far as we can tell, no one of the great world religions is salvifically superior to the rest."[4] This is not yet the pluralistic claim – which, recall, was that each religion is on a par with every other with respect to salvation; it is only a claim about the view that those who attempt an investigation of such a question find themselves assenting to. But it is a claim that in Hick's view comports well enough with the pluralistic answer to the question of salvation. If the evidence we have and the work we've done had suggested that Confucians, by and large, are dramatically more loving than Christians, this would have called into question the pluralistic answer rather than provided supportive evidence for it. Hick, moreover, is confident that if we are able to do more empirical work in the line his assumptions suggest, the result we'll get will support the pluralistic response to the question of salvation ever more strongly.

The first thing to note about Hick's position is that it is not really pluralistic, even though this is what he likes to call it. He does not claim that

all religions are equally salvifically effective. Neither, modulating the discussion into an epistemological key, does he claim that we are not in a
position to tell that inhabiting any particular religion is more salvifically
effective than inhabiting any other. Instead, he claims that if we limit our
consideration to "the great traditions" we can't easily tell whether any one
of them is more salvifically effective – more productive of saints or of just
social structures – than any other. The range of religions to be considered
has already been narrowed down. Hick does not want to claim that the
great traditions (Christianity, Buddhism, Islam, and so forth – the textbook
cases) are just as salvifically effective as nonuniversalistic religions whose
principal interest is in the good of the tribe (he often calls these "pre-
axial religions").[5] Neither is he interested in claiming that new religions,
those without much of a track record and with what may seem to be
idiosyncratic ethical teachings, are salvifically on a par with the great traditions. Consider the following passage:

> What however of the lesser traditions, and the new religious movements
> which have sprung up within, say, the last hundred and fifty years – includ-
> ing Bahai, Christian Science, Rissho Koseikai, Soka Gakkai, Tenrikyo, the
> Church of Jesus Christ of Latter Day Saints, Spiritualism, theosophy, the
> Kimbanguist movement, Johrei, the Unification Church . . . ? To what
> extent are these also contexts of salvation/liberation? The same soteriolog-
> ical criterion and the same index of saintliness are valid, but are harder to
> apply to the much slighter data-base presented by such relatively recent phe-
> nomena. Our pluralistic hypothesis does not entail any *a priori* judgment
> concerning the salvific value of these new movements.[6]

Hick is prepared to allow that these new movements may turn out not
to be "contexts of salvation/liberation" – and in the case of movements
like Aum Shinrikyo, or the Heaven's Gate Community, whose members
committed suicide for religious reasons in California in 1997, it would be
difficult for him to argue that they are. The teachings of such groups sometimes explicitly recommend murder or suicide; and this is not easily compatible with Hick's own emphasis on the golden rule as the ethical core
of the teachings of all the great traditions. Hick could have made his claim
about salvific effectiveness apply to all religions – and as a result be genuinely pluralistic in the sense given to that term here – only by defining
the term religion so that it would apply only to the forms of life that
appear approximately to meet his ethical criteria. But he chooses not to
do this, and as a result is forced to acknowledge the possibility that some
religious forms of life may be less productive of saints and just social struc-

tures than others. He says little about the fairly good empirical evidence we have about the results of serious practice as a member of Aum Shinrikyo or Heaven's Gate; if he had, he would have been forced to be more explicit than he is about the fact that not all religions are equally salvifically efficacious (on his understanding of salvation).

The features of Hick's position just indicated are illustrative of a general feature of pluralistic responses to the question of salvation – or at least of those that employ a substantive understanding of what salvation is, even when it is as attenuated as Hick's idea of transformation from self-centeredness to Reality-centeredness. It is that such responses can maintain themselves only by using a narrow understanding of religion. They can, that is, be plausible only if they limit the religions they consider to those whose substantive teachings about the proper end of human life are significantly like theirs. To the extent that they permit forms of life with very different understandings to be included under the category of religion, they will become implausible.

Those who use a formal understanding of salvation like the one in play in this book are not subject to this difficulty. I understand salvation to mean whatever end (goal, purpose, culmination) of human life is claimed by a religious community to be final and unsurpassable. These ends may be substantively very different. Some religions may envisage a racially-separated paradise, as the Nation of Islam (a quasi-Islamic movement that began in the United States in the twentieth century) appears to do; others might imagine a blissful embodied life in eternity, face to face with God, as Catholic Christians do; yet others might imagine a disembodied translation to the company of extra-terrestrials in spaceships, as the Heaven's Gate community apparently did. On such an understanding of salvation (and its correspondingly formal understanding of religion, as set forth in section 1.2) it is possible to claim that every religion is equally salvifically effective. This would mean that inhabiting any religion is efficacious in producing the salvation envisaged and promised by that religion, and that all religions are on a salvific par in that sense. This is not a position I'd wish to defend; but if you should want to work out a pluralist response to the question of salvation, this is probably the route to take. It lacks the inner conceptual difficulties that Hick's version of pluralism cannot avoid.

But there is more to say about Hick's limited version of pluralism with respect to salvation. Suppose we grant him his claim that all the great traditions might be on a par with respect to transforming their inhabitants from self- to Reality-centeredness; suppose we drop the epistemic modesty and grant him the much stronger claim that they actually are on a par; suppose we grant, in addition, his view that all the great traditions do offer an ethical teaching whose core may be expressed in the golden rule. (I don't in fact think that any of these claims are true; but granting them for argument's sake will permit us to see another kind of difficulty with Hick's position.) If all this is granted, it still doesn't follow that a pluralistic response to the question of salvation is the correct one.

To see this, imagine a religion that has the properties just mentioned: it transforms its inhabitants from self- to Reality-centeredness and propounds a Hickian ethic of niceness to others. But this religion teaches that what Hick takes to be the marks of the saved (principally ethical transformation) in fact have nothing to do with salvation. Salvation, rather, is understood to be a condition which no marks, ethical or otherwise, permit us to infer. You may be a saintly person; but this says nothing about whether you're saved. God's ways, perhaps, are mysterious and unpredictable. Perhaps God looks for an inner state – a broken and contrite heart – that is not outwardly evident as a proper condition for salvation, and perhaps it is just and only those with a broken and contrite heart whom God loves and will save (Jesus, after all, promised paradise to the criminal crucified with him who was contrite and faithful – Luke 23:43).

Hick's understanding of what people progressing toward salvation are like is very different from this (imaginary) religion's understanding, even though the religion has all the marks he suggests belong to one that is salvifically effective for its inhabitants. He will have to say to the doctors and teachers of this religion that they are wrong about what salvation is and about how to determine its presence. For if they are right, his view that it is at least theoretically possible to determine who is saved by appeal to empirical data will have to be abandoned. Hick's quasi-pluralistic view of what produces salvation and how to determine who is saved, is, as this example shows, itself no more obvious than others that are equally compatible with the data to which he appeals. Hick, then, is himself offering a religious, or at least quasi-religious, understanding of what salvation is. There is of course no reason why he should not do so. But if he does, he must also acknowledge that his understanding has no more claim upon those who are religiously alien to him, or upon those who are not religious, than does any other religion-specific understanding of the matter. It is one more religious proposal, another player in the field. The only thing that distinguishes it from the proposals offered by more full-blooded forms of religion (Shi'ite Islam, say; or Calvinist Christianity) is that it is more anemic and less interesting.

Yet another criticism may be offered of Hick's form of the pluralistic response to the question of salvation, even if all his assumptions are allowed. It is an epistemological one. That is, given his own views about how difficult it is to assess the evidence available to us about the transformative efficacy of the great religions, the proper conclusion is that we have no ground upon which to judge that all the great religions are equally transformative, just as we have no ground to judge that they are not. If it is true, as Hick suggests, that the available evidence does not support the idea that any one of the great traditions is more productive of saints or just social structures than any other (and I agree with him that this is true), this supports neither the parity-thesis (*all the great traditions are equally salvifically effective*) nor its contradictory (*it is not the case that all the great traditions are equally salvifically effective*). It supports, rather, the claim *we have no idea whether all the great traditions are or are not equally salvifically effective*.

These criticisms of Hick's form of the pluralistic response to the question of salvation under consideration here (which is, recall, *how may humans realize their proper end?*) can be generalized. Hick understands his semi-pluralist answer to this question to be one based upon, and in theory falsifiable by, evidence. He also uses a substantive understanding of what salvation is. Any attempt at a pluralist answer to the question of salvation with these two characteristics must make a selection among religions and apply the answer only to them; this is because the evidence is clear that not all religions share the same understanding of the proper end of humans, and that the effects wrought by inhabiting different religions are of very different kinds. Therefore, no consistently and fully pluralistic answer to the question of salvation is possible on the basis of Hick's assumptions.

A more fully pluralistic answer could be attempted that denied the relevance of evidence. This would be an approach that affirmed the truth of a fully pluralist answer – belonging to the home religion bears the same relation to the attainment of salvation as does belonging to any alien religion – as something knowable with certainty even in a situation of complete ignorance about the particulars of any alien religion. The most likely version of such an approach will be negatively pluralistic. It appears coherent to say, for instance, that the home religion guarantees to those who belong to it the truth of the following claim: *the attainment of salvation has nothing whatever to do with belonging to any religion*. Perhaps, as I've already suggested, it has only to do with mysterious and unpredictable choices made by God; or with unknowable facts about the karmic inheritance of individuals. No actual religion, however, appears to claim this.

Could there coherently be a positively pluralistic response to the question of salvation that denied the relevance of evidence? I think there could, though again it does not appear to be offered by any actual religion. It would run something like this. The home religion might have among its doctrines the claim that, over the long haul, each and every religious form of life will have just the same effects upon its inhabitants: they will all be brought to the same proper end, the end that everyone should want, and it is the fact that they belong to a religion that will bring them there. The home religion might also teach that evidence to the contrary (evidence, perhaps, that different religions appear to be leading those who belong to them in very different directions, having deeply different effects upon them) need not be seen as calling this claim into question. Something will depend here upon how the phrase "the long haul" is understood. If the haul is very long, it might reasonably be said that apparent divergences now will, over time, come to converge; and that if the claim about identity of effect is really among the central deliverances of the home religion, it ought to be assented to (or at least accepted) in any case, without respect to what the evidence is.

This is probably the best that can be done with pluralism as a response to the question about salvation. It is not a response of much importance to religious people because it is typical of such people, as I've indicated, to judge that belonging to the home religion is positively connected in some way (usually causally) to the attainment of salvation, and to conclude from this that the home religion provides those who belong to it some advantages with respect to the attainment of salvation. The recent popularity of semi-pluralistic responses to the question like that offered by Hick has more to do with a perceived need to be tolerant and accommodating and to repent of colonialism and evangelism than it has to do with a serious attempt to understand what it is like to be religious. There are deep connections here with the pull toward privatizing religion discussed in section 3.4.

## 5.2 Exclusivism

Exclusivism, as a response to the question of how humans realize their proper end, is more likely than pluralism to be acceptable and interesting to religious people. Exclusivists on this matter assert at least the following core claim: *belonging to the home religion is necessary for salvation.* This, as we've seen, is to deny salvific efficacy to any alien religion. But it is not to assert salvific sufficiency to the home religion; exclusivists may or may not add to the core claim the view that *belonging to the home religion is sufficient for salvation*. I'll discuss exclusivism only in terms of its claim as to the necessity of belonging to the home religion for the attainment of salvation.

Exclusivism is difficult to accept or even to give a serious hearing for many late-modern inhabitants of forms of political and economic life that understand choice, preference, and tolerance as unsurpassable values. Such inhabitants – and it's likely enough that you, the reader of this book, are among them – tend to resist the immediate implication of exclusivism, which is that everyone who does not belong to the home religion must thereby inevitably fail to attain what everyone should want, the proper end of all humans. You might think, for example, that, since people's religion is usually given to them by causes beyond their control (parents, teachers, local culture), it is unfair that their eternal destiny should depend upon it. Or you might think it so obvious that nothing of deep importance to anyone can really be beyond their control that when you come across a view (like exclusivism) that claims just this, and does so in very stark terms, the fact that it makes such a claim is enough to make you reject it.

An explicitly Christian form of exclusivism with respect to salvation would say that all non-Christians (and so all faithful religious people who are not Christian) are damned to eternal separation from God. An explicitly Buddhist form of the same view would say that all non-Buddhists (and so all faithful religious people who are not Buddhist) are damned to eternal rebirth and redeath in the agonizing cycles of samsara. These are uncomfortable views, but they are what exclusivism immediately suggests.

This fact that exclusivism with respect to salvation is repugnant to many well-educated early twenty-first century Americans (to habitual readers of the *New York Times*, for example) says nothing about whether the view can be coherently stated, much less about whether there are good reasons for anyone to accept it. In order to explore these questions it will be useful to have an example of a defense of exclusivism with respect to salvation before us, as well as some actual instance of a critique of the position. For the former I choose the Swiss Protestant theologian Karl Barth (1886–1968); and for the latter the American Protestant theologian Schubert Ogden (1928– ). The thought of each man is complex and treats virtually every theological topic. I therefore can't hope to do justice to either man's work here, even on the small topic of interest to this book. A suggestive sketch is all that can be hoped for.

Central to Barth's thought is a complex view of what religion is.[7] The first element in this view is that religion is a human activity, a form of culture that we construct for ourselves. And since, for Barth, everything that we do for ourselves, apart from God, is tainted by idolatry and the absence of faith, it follows that religion must be of this sort, too.[8] It's not something that God does for us; it's something that we do for ourselves. Religion is therefore understood by Barth as piety,[9] which is not intended as a compliment. It means that religion is always and necessarily a self-contradictory and idolatrous human construction, something that builds a golden calf with human effort rather than responding to the living God with faith. It is something weak, contingent, and conditioned by accidental cultural and historical particularities.[10] This, of course, is a Christian-theological understanding of religion, one constructed on the basis of specifically Christian categories – such as thinking of human nature as fallen. Barth is clear that this is so, and he takes it to be perfectly proper to proceed in this way. He thinks that Christians ought to begin thinking about religion (as indeed about everything else) as Christians, which means by using explicitly Christian theological views. (There are implications here for the discussion of epistemic confidence in chapter 3.)

Barth opposes to religion, so understood, revelation. This is something that God freely does, an action of God's that judges, contradicts, and condemns all human activity undertaken apart from God – including religious activity.[11] This free, revelatory self-giving of God judges and condemns all religiosity, all human piety, including the Christian versions of it. Insofar as the Christian religion is simply something that we humans do, it, like all alien religions, is nothing more than idolatry, something to be judged and rejected by God. Christianity is not, for Barth, intrinsically superior to any other religion; instead, it is on a par with them as being opposed to and contradicted by revelation.

But – and here is the characteristically Barthian paradox – Christianity has been chosen by God as the locus of revelation, the place in human history where God chooses (has chosen and will continue to choose) to reveal himself to us. As he says:

> Revelation singles out the Church as the *locus* of true religion. But this does not mean that the Christian religion as such is the fulfilled nature of human religion. It does not mean that the Christian religion is the true religion, fundamentally superior to all other religions. We can never stress too much the connexion between the truth of the Christian religion and the grace of revelation. We have to give particular emphasis to the fact that through

grace the Church lives by grace, and to that extent it is the *locus* of true religion.[12]

The paradox then is that Christianity (the home religion for Barth, of course) both is and is not the true religion. It is because God has chosen it, made its history and its forms the sphere or locus of his action; and it is not because it, like all religions, is a humanly-constructed idol. Barth's emphasis on grace (God's free act) ties the two halves of the paradox together. God transforms an idol into a means of salvation; but without God's free choice to do so, it would remain an idol. What, then, does this view of Christianity mean with respect to the question of whether belonging to Christianity, being a Christian, is necessary for salvation? Briefly, and rather too simply, the properly Barthian answer hinges upon just how the locution *being a Christian* is understood. If it's understood chiefly or solely in terms of what Christians do (their piety, their institutional forms, their beliefs, their hopes, desires, and thoughts), then it is related only negatively to salvation, for on this understanding to be a Christian is to be an idolater, just as much and in just the same way as is to be an inhabitant of an alien religion. But if it's understood chiefly or solely in terms of a response of faith to what God has done and is doing, a grateful and joyful acceptance of God's choice of the Church as the place where his grace is available,[13] then it is indeed a necessary condition for salvation, a condition that God's grace ensures can be found nowhere else. "Revelation," as Barth says, "can adopt religion and mark it off as true religion."[14] He goes on:

> And it not only can. How do we come to assert that it can, if it has not already done so? There is a true religion: just as there are justified sinners. If we abide strictly by that analogy – and we are dealing not merely with an analogy, but in a comprehensive sense with the thing itself – we need have no hesitation in saying that the Christian religion is the true religion.[15]

Notice the definite article (present in the German original as well as in the English translation quoted): Barth means not just that Christianity is *a* true religion; he means that it, and it alone (with some complications and qualifications about Judaism that I won't here go into), is *the* true religion, and therefore that it and it alone is where God's grace is to be found, and where salvation is available. The analogy with justified sinners is important and helpful, too. Sinners, in Christian thought, are those who have done what God does not want, what opposes God. They are also those who can, by themselves, do nothing about this situation; their own sin leaves them in a condition of helpless and hopeless opposition to God. In this they are like the religions (including Christianity considered simply as such): in a condition of idolatrous opposition to grace. But sinners can be justified by God's freely-offered (graceful) forgiveness. They don't thereby cease to be sinners; but they do become forgiven sinners. So also for Christianity-as-a-religion: by God's graceful choice (election) of it, it becomes not just a humanly constructed artifact, not just religion-as-idol (though still always that as well), but also a realm of grace. Given, also, that salvation depends upon grace, Barth is an exclusivist with respect to salvation in the sense given to that position here.

It is important to notice that Barth is an exclusivist with respect to salvation on theological grounds, which is to say that he is so because he takes a proper understanding of Christianity to require this position. He is not interested in trying to convince non-Christians that Christianity is the only true religion, and so he does not offer arguments to this effect that are likely to have much meaning or persuasive power for those not already thinking theologically as Christians. His exclusivism follows and flows out from his particular understanding of Christianity, and this is a general feature of religion-specific exclusivisms. Buddhist or Islamic exclusivisms will typically share it. If such versions of exclusivism are accepted or acceptable, it will be because the more general and basic features of the doctrines and teachings of the religion that produces them are acceptable. This is a structural feature of most religion-specific responses to the conceptual questions raised by knowledge of religious diversity, one by now familiar.

Let's now ask what objections may be brought against a Barthian exclusivism – and, more generally, against structurally similar forms of religion-specific exclusivism. You should keep in mind while thinking about this that exclusivism is, unlike pluralism, a position widely held by religious people because it tends to flow naturally from the nature of religious commitment. That it stands in deep tension with the values of contemporary democratic polities should only make it more interesting.

There are two widely-canvassed kinds of objection to these kinds of exclusivism. The first is broadly epistemological, the second broadly ethical. I'll say a few words about each in turn.

Schubert Ogden will be helpful in putting the epistemological objection to exclusivism as clearly as possible.[16] Ogden understands exclusivism to be the view that "Christianity is the only true religion . . . [and] that Christians alone, as participants in this religion through their membership in the visible church, obtain the salvation that God established it to mediate."[17] Ogden's is thus an understanding of the position roughly similar to the one offered in this chapter. Ogden offers a number of reasons for rejecting the exclusivist claim, only one of which, a fundamentally epistemological reason, will be of interest here. He says that exclusivism, so understood, must be rejected because it cannot meet the credibility criterion, a criterion which any claim at all must meet in order to be worthy of assent. What is the credibility criterion? Well, in Ogden's words it's the criterion that asks whether a particular claim can meet "the conditions of truth that are everywhere given with existence itself."[18] And what are these? Matters become a little foggy here at the strictly theoretical level, but it's fairly easy to see what Ogden means when he applies the credibility criterion to exclusivism. Here's what he says:

> Nothing that even a Christian could experience would warrant holding that the way in which she or he and other Christians have been given the possibility of salvation is the only way in which it has been or can be given . . . There would be no way, even in principle, of ever verifying it in terms of common human experience and reason, since no human experience could show that God has not given or cannot give the possibility of salvation in some other way.[19]

The credibility criterion seems, if this example of its application is any guide, to require verification by experience. The idea seems to be that no belief ought to be held if it cannot be verified (in principle if not in practice) by some specifiable human experience that anyone could (in principle) have. Ogden does not make clear here (or anywhere else that I have come across) just what counts as verification by experience. It is not accidental that he does not, for it turns out to be extremely difficult to do so in any useful way. The following example may help to show why.

What experience does (or could) verify my belief that there are human beings other than myself? Perhaps seeing or talking with what appear to me to be such. But then we have a weak verification criterion, for of course it remains possible that what appear to me to be the humans with whom I converse are figments of my imagination or the product of faulty patterns of synaptic firing in my brain. That I take them not to be (and that I am right to do so) is intimately connected with my belief that there are in fact human beings other than myself (just as this belief is intimately connected with its seeming to me that I see and talk with such beings). But if this is what Ogden has in mind, then of course there are many experiences that could verify exclusivism: its seeming to me that I am being told by God that it is true, for instance; or its being taught to me by the Church. Here too we have instances of the same logical kind, of a particular belief (that exclusivism is true) being intimately connected with and complexly supported by an experience (of its seeming to me that God says such-and-such, or that the Church teaches such-and-such). If Ogden wants a closer relation between experience and claim than this – perhaps that the experience in question entails the truth of the claim – he will, I think, have to say that beliefs such as *there are human persons other than me* and *the sun will rise tomorrow* are in just the same epistemic case as he takes exclusivism to be. And this, I take it, is not a desirable conclusion.

The theory of knowledge implied by Ogden's epistemic rejection of exclusivism is not one that can easily be defended, and certainly not one whose truth ought to be assumed in rejecting a position as complicated and interesting as exclusivism. Some alternative epistemologies are explored in chapter 3; most of those don't require the rejection of exclusivism for the epistemic reasons given by Ogden in his application of the credibility criterion to it. Ogden's rejection of exclusivism is, though, representative of many other (often inchoate) kinds of uneasiness with exclusivism as a position. Underlying most of them is the correct perception that religious exclusivists seem (to the nonreligious) all to be in the same boat, epistemically speaking. That is, they all offer reasons for exclusivism that (like Barth's) are religion-specific and that have no persuasive purchase upon the alien, whether religious or not. Moving from this worry to the conclusion that the application of epistemic principles (like Ogden's *believe only what's accessible to common human experience and reason*) can by itself rule out the propriety of assenting to exclusivism (or its like) is tempting, natural – and quite mistaken. Again, the discussion in chapter 3 (especially sections 3.3 and 3.5) will show why. Ogden-like epistemological worries about exclusivism do not, therefore, need to be taken very seriously. This is perfectly compatible with saying that exclusivism is false in any or all of its particular forms; it is only to say that there's no good reason to rule out in principle the propriety of anyone's holding it.

But not all worries about exclusivism are epistemological. Some are ethical, and to these I now turn.

Those who put the ethical objections tend to be worried about what seems at first blush to be the inevitable result of exclusivisms of the kind canvassed, which is that vast numbers of people will not attain their proper ends – will be damned or otherwise condemned to long-term unpleasantness. Nonreligious people are perhaps most often worried about this (or say they are): it seems to them intolerant, judgmental, antidemocratic, opposed to the free market, and in other ways simply unacceptable. But religious people are often worried about it, too. Some Christians, Jews, and Muslims, for instance (though more Christians than Jews or Muslims) think it improper to worship a God who would make a world such that the majority of people in it cannot realize their proper ends through no apparent fault of their own. Some of them also think that there are strands of thought within Christianity (or Judaism, or Islam) that call such a view into question: strands, perhaps, that emphasize God's universal salvific will, or God's universal and profound compassion.

Two responses are possible to this kind of objection. The first is that restrictivism – the position that not everyone will attain their proper end – does not follow immediately from exclusivism, and may indeed not be at all closely related to it. You can, that is, be an exclusivist and yet not think that some are inevitably damned. Barth himself affirmed exclusivism, as we've seen, and yet rejected restrictivism (showing that he rejected restrictivism would take me too far afield, so I'll have to content myself with the bare affirmation that he did). But how is this possible? Briefly, the argument from exclusivism to restrictivism would go like this: belonging to the home religion is necessary for salvation; some do not belong to the home religion; therefore, some are not saved. The strategy for avoiding this conclusion upon the basis of the first premise is to look more closely at the second premise, which is that some do not belong to the home religion. At first blush, this seems obviously true. Some are not (now) Christian; some are not (now) Buddhist; and so on. But, the argument will go, it doesn't follow from the fact that you don't now belong to the home religion that you never will. You may come to belong to it at some time in the future. And so the argument ought be recast to read: belonging to the home religion at some time is necessary for salvation; some will never belong to the home religion; and so some will never be saved.

But now the second premise – some will never belong to the home religion – is much less obviously true. Those who don't belong to it now may come to do so, and in virtue of coming to do so may be saved. Life is, after all, long, and conversion always a possibility. But now you might object that some die without being converted; aren't they, even on the new argument, incapable of being saved? Well, not unless you think that chances to belong to the home religion end with death. And this is not at all an obvious thing to think. Buddhists and Hindus, for instance,

certainly don't think it, since they have among their teachings the claim
that all people have many lives. Some Christians, too, don't think it: the
idea that there is a condition called purgatory that follows upon death, in
which there are more chances of various sorts is widely held by Christians, especially Catholic Christians.[20] And there are Protestant versions of
such a position, as well.

But even if you do think, whether as a Christian or otherwise, that
opportunities to belong to the home religion end with death – which
would seem to mean that if you haven't come to belong to it by then,
and if so coming is necessary for salvation, then there's no way you can
be saved – it doesn't immediately follow that some are not saved. This
would only follow if it is true that some do not belong to the home religion at death. There are certainly some understandings of what it means
to belong to the home religion on which this is true. Suppose, for
example, you're a Christian and you think that an essential element of
belonging to Christianity is having freely and consciously accepted baptism
in the name of God the Father, God the Son, and God the Holy Ghost.
On such an understanding, it is clearly true that some die without belonging to Christianity. Or, suppose you're a Buddhist and you think it intrinsic to belonging to Buddhism that you know and can recite the triple
refuge (I take refuge in the Buddha/I take refuge in his doctrine/I take
refuge in his monastic community). On this understanding, too, it follows
immediately by observation and inference that some die without belonging to Buddhism. But there are understandings of belonging to the home
religion on which no such thing follows. Suppose, for example, you think
that it suffices to belong to Christianity that you are partly and imper-
fectly aware of the triune God's nature and demands upon you, and that
you respond to these demands with faith. On this understanding it will
be much harder to be sure whether some die without belonging to Christianity: faith, like paternity, is not straightforwardly a matter of observation; in this it differs from confession. And so on this understanding (and
there are many like it, including some held and defended by religious
people) restrictivism does not follow immediately or obviously from exclusivism. Deciding whether restrictivism does so follow in a particular case
will therefore always require delicate and complex decisions by religious
people about what it means to belong to the home religion, decisions that
carry with them many other assumptions and entailments.

Moves of the kind briefly mentioned in the preceding paragraph soften
the immediate bite of exclusivism as a response to the question of salvation by correspondingly softening (or at least making more epistemically

inaccessible) the criteria that define belonging to the home religion. This in turn moves the position toward inclusivism, the third kind of response to the question of salvation. I'll take this up again in section 5.3.

Restrictivism does not, then, immediately and necessarily follow from exclusivism with respect to salvation. This is the first kind of response to those with ethical worries about restrictivism and tendencies to think that it does rapidly and inevitably follow from exclusivism. But this response might seem to agree with those who offer the criticism (whether for religious or nonreligious reasons) that restrictivism, if it did follow, could not be defended for ethical reasons. The second mode of responding to ethically-motivated critics of exclusivism is to deny that restrictivism is incapable of defense, and to affirm instead that there's nothing obviously wrong with restrictivism in some of its forms. I'll return to this matter in the discussion of restrictivism and inclusivism in section 5.4.

In sum: Exclusivism will tend to be offered by the religiously committed as a response to the question of how humans realize their proper ends; further, those who offer it will tend to have a high degree of epistemic confidence in the doctrines and teachings of the home religion, and will tend to be inclusivist (when they are not incoherently exclusivist) on the question of truth. An important distinction is to be noted between exclusivism on the question of truth, which (I observed in section 2.7) is very difficult to state coherently and largely unpalatable to religious people; and exclusivism on the question of salvation, which can be stated coherently (I've tried to do so in this section), and which has a powerful fascination for at least some of the religiously committed.

## 5.3 Inclusivism

Inclusivism is, in its deep logical structure, either simply a form of exclusivism or a position closely derived from it. Both positions answer the question of how humans realize their proper end by claiming that belonging to the home religion provides an advantage to be had in no other way. Exclusivism, as we've seen, makes belonging to the home religion essential for salvation, but it also, in some of its variants, offers a relaxed understanding of what it might mean to belong to the home religion. Inclusivism in its most common form simply makes this relaxed understanding explicit by saying that consciously (publicly, explicitly) belonging to the home religion is not necessary for salvation, that belonging to an alien religion may suffice, and that this is so because the sincere and faithful practitioner of an alien religion is in fact participating in the home religion – though implicitly and anonymously, without knowing it. The core idea here is that of anonymous participation.

This kind of answer to the question of salvation is also attractive to many religious people. Like the exclusivist answer, it preserves the non-negotiable unsurpassability of the home religion, and is as a result largely adequate to one of the central elements of being religious. But it raises fewer ethical difficulties because it distances itself from restrictivism.

A brief sketch of a Buddhist version of this kind of inclusivism would go like this. First, explicit understanding of Buddhist doctrine, coupled with a sincere and long-term attempt to order your life in accord with that doctrine, is the best possible means for bringing you to your proper end – which is, in brief, the cessation of greed, hatred, and delusion and the concomitant attainment of Buddhahood. But insofar as what is recommended and taught by an alien religion accords with what is recommended and taught by Buddhism, serious practitioners of the alien religion are in fact practicing Buddhism (in a limited and imperfect way, of course) even though they don't know it. Such practitioners are, we might say, anonymous Buddhists. The Buddhist inclusivist will then add that it is possible that the anonymous Buddhist be saved even if she never comes to have explicit knowledge of anything Buddhist.

Buddhist inclusivists are likely to add to the sketch just given that an anonymous Buddhist will typically, after a lifetime or several of inhabiting an alien religion, be born into a life in which she can come to an explicit understanding of Buddhist doctrine and practice. This is an easy move for Buddhists to make because they usually hold it as axiomatic that each of us has many lives (often uncountably many), and that the situation into which we are born when we enter upon a new life is deeply affected, causally, by what we have done in previous lives. This is why it will be normal for anonymous Buddhists to become explicit and conscious ones as a result of their sincere practice in the right sort of alien religion. Such a move is a little more difficult (though not by any means impossible) for those religions whose doctrines limit us to one life.

This Buddhist example also nicely shows how easily inclusivism becomes indistinguishable from exclusivism. If public and explicit understanding of the home religion's doctrine and practice is required before salvation can be attained (as the most common Buddhist versions of inclusivism will say), then we have a version of exclusivism, even though one that permits an approach to be made to the home religion by way of belonging to an alien one. But if salvation can be had without such public and explicit understanding ever occurring, then we have inclusivism in the strict sense. Whether inclusivism in the strict sense or inclusivism in the more or less exclusivist sense is preferred will depend, for religious people, on how the particular demands of the home religion are understood. Strict inclusivists must read the home religion in such a way that explicit knowledge and confession of its particulars is not necessary for salvation; and in so doing they must call into question the salvific importance of knowing and confessing these particulars, which is usually a difficulty for religious people; however, in being strictly inclusivist they are easily able to avoid restrictivism, and this is usually a benefit for religious people.

Christians have been divided about these matters, and there are certainly elements (biblical, creedal, liturgical) in Christianity that can be called upon to support both sides of the question. A full Christian argument as to the relative benefits of strict inclusivism and exclusivism would require detailed treatment of all these elements, and this in turn would require the writing of several more books. I shall only register my opinion that the grammar and syntax of orthodox Christian thought strongly suggests that some version of exclusivism (in the sense defined and discussed in section 5.2) must be affirmed; and that restrictivism (at least in its more extreme versions) must simultaneously be denied. Since Christians who reject exclusivism on salvation usually do so because they're worried about restrictivism, seeing that affirming exclusivism need not require assenting to restrictivism (as already suggested in section 5.2) should remove the chief motive for teaching strict inclusivism – always assuming that exclusivism and universalism can coherently be held together.

In order to see more clearly how all this might go, some further discussion of restrictivism and universalism is in order. These positions, recall, are answers to the question of who is saved; pluralism, exclusivism, and inclusivism are answers to the question of how humans may realize their proper end. Keeping the differences between these two questions in mind will help you again to see that it is possible to hold together, for example, exclusivism and universalism, and that restrictivism is not entailed by exclusivism.

## 5.4 Restrictivism and Universalism

The core claim of restrictivism is: *not all will be saved*, which is the same as to say *some will not be saved*. There are varieties of restrictivism and they are most easily differentiated by paying attention to the mode under which the core claim is asserted. Some restrictivists assert the core claim as possible: it picks out, they say, a state of affairs that might obtain, which is to say a state of affairs that can coherently be supposed either to obtain or not to obtain. Some restrictivists among those who so understand the core claim may go on to say that it picks out an actual state of affairs – that it not only might be the case that some will not be saved, but that it actually is the case that some are not saved. Other restrictivists may understand the core claim differently, to pick out a state of affairs that must obtain, that can't coherently be supposed not to. Naturally, restrictivists of this stripe must also think that it actually is the case that some will not be saved, since this follows from the claim's necessity. Differences between possibilists who are also actualists about restrictivism and possibilists who are not, as well as those between both of these and restrictivist necessitarians, will usually follow from differences in the teachings and doctrines of the home religion, differences that seem to require one position or the other. Some examples will be before us in a moment.

The core claim of universalism is the contradictory of restrictivism's core claim. It is the claim *all will be saved*, which has as its equivalent *there is no one who will not be saved*. It is possible to assert this claim, too, as picking out a state of affairs that necessarily must (and therefore does) obtain; it is also possible to assert it as a possibility, as something that may or may not obtain. On this second understanding, the universalist asserts *it is possible that all will be saved*. This is equivalent to *it is possible that some will not be saved*, which is the possibilist reading of restrictivism's central claim. The two positions merge at this point; those who hold either restrictivism or universalism as possibilities are thereby committed to holding that the other view also picks out a possible state of affairs. This is because the core claim of restrictivism is the complement of the core claim of universalism.

Those who hold that either restrictivism or universalism is true – that it picks out a state of affairs that obtains, whether necessarily or contingently – will usually be epistemic optimists with a good deal of confidence in particular interpretations of the doctrine and teaching of the home religion. That is, they will take it that there is something about the teaching or doctrine of the home religion that clearly shows restrictivism (or universalism) to be true, and therefore shows its acceptance to be required by those who belong to the home religion. Those who hold that both of these views are possible will typically find themselves less strongly impelled than are the actualist epistemic optimists by anything in the home religion's teachings to assert the truth of one or the other. The pattern of epistemic optimism with respect to a particular understanding of the home religion's doctrine is evident in the following example of Buddhist restrictivism.

Many Buddhists think that it is necessarily the case that samsara – the cycle of rebirth, redeath, and suffering upon the wheel of which we are all bound (and not only we humans but also all sentient beings) – will never have a final end. This is because a final end to samsara would mean that all sentient beings had finally and irreversibly left suffering behind by definitively extinguishing the desires and passions that are its sole cause. It would mean that all sentient beings had left the burning lake of samsara for the cool pond of nirvana. And this in turn would mean that Buddhas have nothing left to do, for the action of Buddhas is defined (by those who follow this line) exclusively in terms of what they do for suffering sentient beings – and so if there are no suffering sentient beings, it follows that there is nothing for them to do. They become otiose. And since it is axiomatic for some Buddhists that this is not a state that Buddhas can ever be in, it follows that no state of affairs requiring it could ever obtain. This in turn means that samsara will never end.

This position is not yet restrictivism because it does not entail *some will not be saved*; it entails only *there will always be some who are not yet saved*. But some Buddhists understand the necessity of samsara's endlessness by postulating a category of sentient beings called the *icchantikas* ("desirers") – those who will endlessly and continuously be desiring, and as a result endlessly and continuously suffering.[21] These sentient beings, by definition, will never attain nirvana; they are restrictivism's "some who will never be saved." Buddhists who hold a view of this sort are restrictivists, and they think that restrictivism necessarily holds, that it cannot not hold. Furthermore, as is normal for a religion-specific view of this sort, this Buddhist version of restrictivism is derived directly from a particular understanding of some of Buddhism's doctrines and teachings, an understanding that may not be shared by all Buddhists.

I've said that the Buddhist view just sketched is a minority view. This also means that it is a controversial view in the sense that many Buddhists find deep (and deeply Buddhist) reasons for disagreeing with it. In this, most Christian views about restrictivism and universalism are like it: there is no dominant Christian view on the matter, and any propounded by Christians as the properly Christian view on the question (the question, recall, is *who is saved?*) is inevitably and directly met by Christian counter-arguments. I'll conclude by offering a brief sketch of how Christian thinking about this matter might go; the sketch will include signals as to the main controversial points, but you should bear in mind that almost every point in it is controversial. It may, indeed, be a generalizable feature of answers to the questions of salvation that they are controversial in this sense, and if this is so it's likely to be because few religions are centrally concerned to give answers to them, and so any particular religion will make more than one answer relatively easy to defend.

Christian thinking about the questions of salvation should begin by affirming exclusivism. This is the view, recall, that makes belonging to the home religion (Christianity in this case, and from now on I'll abandon the religion-neutral terminology) necessary for salvation. This, as I've already suggested, can reasonably be regarded as a central claim of Christianity, one the abandonment of which causes much else in it to cease to make sense. I don't specify any particular way in which "belonging to" must be understood, other than to rule out understanding it as requiring explicit, publicly-observable adherence. Understanding it in that way creates too many difficulties and is not sufficiently warranted by the tradition.

"Belonging to Christianity" means, then, something like being rightly related by faith to the God of Jesus Christ; it need not require being able to identify God under just this description, but it does require that insofar as someone is a recipient of God's grace – which is, for Christians, in the end the only way that salvation can be had – this grace is made available through Jesus Christ. So understanding what it is to belong to Christianity is intended to safeguard the centrality of what God has done in Christ, while not requiring any particular level of explicit knowledge or understanding of this. This is not to say that such knowledge or understanding is unimportant or irrelevant to salvation; it is only to say that Christians ought not to think that they can perform the difficult and theologically dubious task of saying just how much explicit knowledge and understanding is necessary in order for salvation to be possible.

I begin, then, with an affirmation of exclusivism, though one with a deliberately relaxed understanding of what "belonging to Christianity" means.

The second move is to affirm that, from a Christian point of view, both restrictivism and universalism are possible answers to the question of who is saved. The former is possible because of human freedom: Christians ought not say (though some have) that anyone's salvation (or damnation) is wrought independently of their own free assent to (or denial of) what God does in freely offering them salvation.[22] This then means that any

particular person can always refuse God's offer of salvation, and in so refusing not accept the offer of grace from which alone salvation comes. And
if even one person consistently and repeatedly does so for all eternity, or
until opportunities to accept God's freely given offer of salvation come to
an end (whichever of these two should come first), then restrictivism turns
out to be true.

This way of putting the possibility of restrictivism is intended to remain
neutral as to when opportunities to accept God's grace cease, but it does
claim that there is such a point, a point beyond which the narrative of
every individual's pilgrim's progress ceases to be told. When this narrative
ceases, nothing new can happen: you'll remain as you are with respect to
what, for Christians, is the most important matter of all, which is your
relation to God. Some will say, as we've already had occasion to note, that
the narrative (and with it, further opportunities to accept God's grace)
ceases at the death of the body, and that therefore the condition you're in
at that point (the two possibilities usually canvassed being "saved" and
"damned," with a third sometimes being added – extinct, out of existence;
but this third possibility, if it's a real one, I subsume under the second,
understanding "damned" to mean "not having realized your proper end")
is the condition you'll remain in for ever. Others will say that this isn't
obvious, and that perhaps there are post-mortem possibilities to accept
God's grace. Whichever position is taken on this (and I strongly incline
toward the latter), the logic of restrictivism's possibility remains the same:
it is that since God will not compel acceptance of grace (if he did it
wouldn't be grace), anyone can at any time refuse it; and that there will
come a time at which new opportunities to refuse or accept cease to
occur, a time at which you've been irrevocably conformed to salvation or
to its absence.

The logic of restrictivism as a possibility is also the logic of universalism as a possibility. It must be, since the two views are the same. But while
the possibility of restrictivism's truth is largely grounded, for Christians,
upon a particular understanding of human freedom, the possibility of universalism's truth is largely grounded upon a particular understanding of
God's passionate desire for the salvation of everyone. To explain what this
means and why Christians must (or ought; some have failed to get even
this straight) think it would require more strictly Christian theology than
is appropriate for a book of this sort. I'll simply assert it as axiomatic for
Christians, and as the view that ought to be the principal motivation for
the Christian assertion of universalism's possibility. God's offer of salvific

grace cannot fail and is of universal scope; this is what makes universalism possible. But it can be refused; and this is what makes restrictivism possible.

This is a bare-bones account of a Christian response to the questions of salvation. It does not require that Christians know which of the two possibilities (restrictivism and universalism) will turn out to be true (of course, if even one person is already irretrievably damned, this means that restrictivism is already true); it requires only that they affirm the possibility of both. But this leaves open the question of whether Christians can in fact know which of these two possibilities is actual. I do not think they can. Possessing such knowledge would require knowing that some particular person is damned, and this in turn would require knowing things about that person and his relation to God that cannot, in principle, be known with certainty by anyone other than the person concerned – and in some cases not even by him. Short of such knowledge, no one can know whether restrictivism is more than a possibility, which also means that no one can know whether universalism is more than a possibility. We are, of course, free if we like to make probabilistic judgments about the damnation of particular individuals – either those whom we know, or historical figures. But making such judgments is unseemly, and likely to be of little use other than to contribute to the possibility of damnation for those who make them.

This position – exclusivism coupled with a possibilist restrictivism – is likely to have two kinds of objection brought against it. Objections of the first kind are of interest only to Christians, and I'll do no more than note their possibility here. These are objections based upon particular readings of the data of the tradition, objections that say the position briefly stated here is contradicted by or does not do justice to something in that data. Perhaps, for instance, there is material in the Bible or in Church teaching that seems to contradict it; or perhaps there's something about the habits of worship or prayer of Christian people that call it into question. Objections of this sort all suggest that the position elucidated isn't properly Christian. There are interesting (and lengthy) debates to be had about such objections; but all I'll do here is say that the position given here appears to me to do as well as its opponents in handling the large range of data from the tradition.

Objections to exclusivism coupled with possibilist restrictivism of the second kind are perhaps not restricted in interest to Christians. They are objections to the internal coherence of the view. Perhaps, it might be said, the position deploys and assumes an understanding of God that is called into question by what it states. There are many such possible objections. I'll note only one as an instance of how such argument goes. For example, perhaps the kind of God whose passionate and universal desire for the salvation of humans cannot also be the kind of God who would permit even the possibility of restrictivism's truth – the possibility, that is, that some people might never realize their proper end, which is what God most deeply wants for us all.

An objection of this sort requires attention to what is meant by saying that God has a universal and passionate desire for universal salvation. What kind of goodness does such a view of God suggest? How can it be made compatible with the action of creating a world in which it is possible that some are damned? – which is what God must have done if the answer to the question of salvation sketched here is the right one. Many (Christian and otherwise) have felt that any God who would do this could not be morally good. And if moral goodness is implied by a passionate desire for universal salvation, then there's a prima facie incoherence in asserting the position sketched in the last few paragraphs. This objection is motivated in part by a deep moral repugnance to the very idea of God's permitting the possibility of damnation, a repugnance that has led some to abandon Christianity and others to reject key elements of its doctrine. John Stuart Mill, in describing the religious opinions of his father, puts this moral repugnance in terms it's hard to better:

> Think (he used to say) of a being who would make a Hell – who would create the human race with the infallible foreknowledge, and therefore with the intention, that the great majority of them were to be consigned to horrible and everlasting torment. The time, I believe, is drawing near when this dreadful conception of an object of worship will no longer be identified with Christianity; and when all persons, with any sense of moral good and evil, will look upon it with the same indignation with which my father regarded it.[23]

This isn't quite the view I've sketched. Mill's father thought, apparently, that Christians (or some of them) are committed to restrictivism's truth, rather than to its possibility. He thought, too, that Christians are committed to a strong view about God's "infallible foreknowledge." And he drew a logically illegitimate connection between knowing that something will happen and intending that it should. But in spite of these differences and difficulties, the questions Mill's father raises are good ones. Responding to them would be a proper exercise in philosophical theology, or philosophy of religion, if you prefer that term. It would require, first, some discussion of what Christians might want to say about God's knowledge, and whether any of these views does result in an understanding of God that makes him responsible, in a moral sense, for the sufferings of those who are not saved. Then it would require work on what might be meant by God's goodness (is this to be understood as significantly like ours, or is it so deeply different from ours that what might be morally indefensible for us is not so for God?), his power (is it possible for God to have created a world in which universalism is not only true, but necessarily so?).

But these are all topics for another occasion; analogues to them of equal depth and interest would be raised by an equally detailed sketch of another religion's response to the questions of salvation. That endless further work of this sort is always suggested and provoked by philosophical exploration of religious diversity is one of the benefits and delights of the topic. It is a benefit and delight that this book has tried to show and to invite you to participate in by further work and thought of your own – perhaps by attention to the questions generated in the preceding paragraph, or to their analogues from another religion. Of such questions there is no end; but of books there must be.

## NOTES

1   John Hick, "Religious Pluralism and Salvation," *Faith and Philosophy* 5 (1988), pp. 365–77, at p. 366.
2   Ibid., p. 367.
3   Ibid.
4   Ibid., p. 369.
5   John Hick, *An Interpretation of Religion: Human Responses to the Transcendent* (New Haven: Yale University Press, 1989), pp. 29–35.
6   Hick, *Interpretation*, pp. 307–8.
7   For this discussion of Karl Barth I've drawn on Garrett Green's "Challenging the Religious Studies Canon: Karl Barth's Theory of Religion," *Journal of Religion* 75/4 (1995), 473–86.
8   Karl Barth, *Church Dogmatics*, vol. I/2, trans. G. T. Thomson and Harold Knight (Edinburgh: T. & T. Clark, 1956), pp. 280, 299, 303.
9   Barth, *Church Dogmatics*, vol. I/2, p. 310.
10  Barth, *Church Dogmatics*, vol. I/2, p. 316. This recalls the discussion in 2.4 of the broadly Kantian views.
11  Barth, *Church Dogmatics*, vol. I/2, p. 295, 299–300, 303 and passim.
12  Ibid., p. 298.
13  Ibid., pp. 344, 353.

14  Ibid., p. 326.
15  Ibid., p. 326.
16  A more detailed version of this analysis may be found in my "How Episte-mology Matters to Theology," *Journal of Religion* 79 (1999), 1–18.
17  Schubert M. Ogden, *Is There Only One True Religion or Are There Many?* (Dallas: Southern Methodist University Press, 1992), p. 29.
18  Schubert M. Ogden, *On Theology* (Dallas: Southern Methodist University Press, 1992), p. 5.
19  Ogden, *Is There Only One?*, p. 44.
20  See, e.g., Joseph A. DiNoia, *The Diversity of Religions: A Christian Perspective* (Washington, D.C.: Catholic University of America Press, 1992), pp. 103–8, for some interesting discussion of this from a Catholic perspective.
21  On the *icchantikas* see Robert E. Buswell and Robert M. Gimello, ed., *Paths to Liberation: The Mārga and its Transformations in Buddhist Thought* (Honolulu: University Press of Hawaii, 1992), pp. 118–23.
22  The formulation offered here would be rejected by some (perhaps by many) Christians, as would the comments about the resistibility of God's grace made in the following paragraph. This intra-Christan controversy unfortunately can't be pursued further here.
23  John Stuart Mill, *Autobiography* (New York: Columbia Press, 1924; first pub-lished [posthumously], 1873), p. 29.

# A Brief Guide to
# Further Reading

There is now a considerable amount of work on religious diversity published each year. Some of it is philosophical, concerned to argue a particular position on one or another of the topics discussed in this book. Some is theological, written from within a particular religious form of life, and often concerned to explain and apply the resources of that particular religion to the topic at hand. And some is empirical or descriptive, concerned to show what a particular form of religious life is like.

The references given in the notes to this book indicate only those works I've quoted or drawn upon directly, and though some of these are important resources for further work in the area (many have their own bibliographies and some have given rise to a lage body of secondary work), they comprise only a small portion of what's available. Consultation of any of the works on the following brief annotated list will provide more resources.

- Gavin D'Costa, ed., *Christian Uniqueness Reconsidered: The Myth of a Pluralistic Theology of Religions* (Maryknoll, New York: Orbis, 1990). A collection of essays responding to the Hick and Knitter volume mentioned below; the contributors argue that claims to uniqueness are deeply woven into the grammar of religious discourse, and that a philosophical defense of some aspects of them can be given.
- Jacques Dupuis, *Toward a Christian Theology of Religious Pluralism* (Maryknoll, New York: Orbis, 1997). A thorough review of the history of Christian thought about religious diversity, together with some constructive (but controversial) theological proposals from a Catholic Christian point of view.
- S. Mark Heim, *Salvations: Truth and Difference in Religion* (Maryknoll, New York: Orbis, 1995). A careful and thorough critique of pluralist

responses to the problems of religious diversity, together with an argument whose conclusion is that different religions propose different ends for their inhabitants, and that a philosophical or theological response to religious diversity must pay attention to this fact.

- John Hick and Paul F. Knitter, eds., *The Myth of Christian Uniqueness: Toward a Pluralistic Theology of Religions* (Maryknoll, New York: Orbis, 1987). A collection of essays by philosophers and theologians arguing against Christian exclusivism on truth and salvation. Responded to in the volume edited by Gavin D'Costa.
- *Faith and Philosophy* Vol. 14, No. 3 (July 1997). This journal is the organ of the Society of Christian Philosophers, and the issue mentioned is devoted to the thought of John Hick. Several of the essays contain useful discussions of and references to recent philosophical work on the problems of religious diversity.
- Francis X. Clooney, *Theology After Vedanta: An Experiment in Comparative Theology* (Albany, New York: State University of New York Press, 1993). An experiment in serious reading of the religious texts of a Hindu school from the standpoint of Catholic Christianity.
- John Sanders, ed., *What About Those Who Have Never Heard? Three Views on the Destiny of the Unevangelized* (Downers Grove, IL: InterVarsity, 1995). A collection of essays by evangelical Protestant Christians on the question of salvation: representative of conservative Protestant opinion in the United States today.
- Jerry L. Walls, *Hell: The Logic of Damnation* (Notre Dame: University of Notre Dame Press, 1992), a Christian defense of some aspects of the doctrine of hell, with attention to the question of salvation posed by religious diversity.

# Index